Imagin

Patchwork

Imaginative Patchwork

Peigi Martin   Susan Young

CHILTON TRADE BOOK PUBLISHING
RADNOR, PENNSYLVANIA

Published in Radnor, Pennsylvania 19089, by Chilton Trade
Book Publishing; in Crow's Nest, New South Wales, Australia,
by Little Hills Press Pty. Ltd.

Designed by Helen Semmler
Edited by Meryl Potter
Illustrations by Jan Düttmer
Production by Vantage Graphics

Photography by Brian Rout, Auckland, and Ian Herbert
Japanese family crests are reproduced by permission from
Encyclopedia Japonica, published by Shogakukan Inc., Japan

© Leman Publications, Inc. Design pp. iii, 79.

Manufactured in Singapore

Library of Congress Cataloging in Publication Data

Martin, Peigi.
  Imaginative patchwork/Peigi Martin, Susan Youg.
    p.   cm.
  Includes index.
  ISBN 0-8019-7897-1
  1. Quilting—Patterns. 2. Patchwork—Patterns.
  I. Young, Susan. II. Title.

TT835.M384 1988   88-23738
                                                   CIP
746.46—dc19

1 2 3 4 5 6 7 8 9 0   7 6 5 4 3 2 1 0 9 8

CONTENTS

BASIC SKILLS

The origins of patchwork, applique and quilting date back to antiquity, but even today these crafts provide us with unlimited scope to fill our leisure time. This book provides a wide range of projects, large and small, with detailed diagrams and instructions and clear photographs to make the construction easy.

The Gallery of Quilts will delight the eye and provide inspiration and a challenge to the more experienced quilter.

Part one describes the basic skills of patchwork and quilting. Many beginning quiltmakers launch themselves into a large and ambitious project at great expense and they are disappointed with the result, or give up before it is completed, because they find that they do not enjoy the technique or find it more difficult than expected. So it is wise to begin with something manageable. Each patchwork and quilting method is explained in detail and a pattern for a cushion is provided. Each cushion is a small and easily mastered lesson in the particular technique, and if they are made in co-ordinating colours, an attractive set will be produced. The methods described are very different and by sampling them all you will find which you prefer. Some will love the precision and relaxation of hand-sewn English piecing, others will find it tedious and time-consuming and feel much happier with machine piecing.

It is important for the survival of quilting that the skills are passed on to the younger generation, so a section dealing with patterns suitable for children to piece is included.

Read through all the instructions for a particular project before starting work.

Throughout the book, important terms are printed in CAPITAL LETTERS. This indicates that the method is described in full elsewhere. Consult the index for the location.

Hand piecing was the traditional method most used by early patchworkers. A small running stitch was used. Closely woven cottons proved to be the most suitable fabrics because they were easy to handle and gave the best results.

For hand piecing, the seam line must be marked on the wrong side of the fabric. The cutting line, ¼ inch (6 millimetres) beyond the seam line, may also be marked, if desired. Use a template cut to the finished size of the patch and place it face down on the wrong side of the fabric. Draw around the template with a pencil, then mark a cutting line that gives a ¼ inch (6 millimetre) seam allowance, or estimate the seam allowance by eye when cutting out. Window templates are ideal for hand piecing because they can be used to mark both the seam and cutting lines. When piecing by hand, the seam line *must* be accurate, because it is used as the guide for the sewing.

After cutting out all the patches you require, lay them out and decide on a logical sewing order. Sew small pieces into larger units that can then be joined in rows or blocks, as shown in diagram 1.

Pick up the first two patches to be joined and place them right sides together. Hand piecing is sewn from seam line to seam line, not from edge to edge. Insert a pin in the end of the seam and check that it has emerged at the end of the seam on the underside. Pin at the other end of the seam, and then at intervals along the seam if necessary. Check that all the pins are accurately placed in the seam line of both pieces of the fabric (diagram 2).

Knot the end of a thread, leaving a short tail. Begin sewing at one end of the seam with one or two backstitches, then sew along the seam with a small running stitch, catching in the tail of the thread. Finish the seam with another backstitch and weave the thread back into the stitches of the seam before clipping (diagram 3). Check that the sewing is accurate and that there are no puckers. Correct any mistakes before continuing.

When the block of patches has been pieced, press it gently on the wrong side, turning the seams to one side. Then press on the right side, making sure that there are no folds against the seam lines.

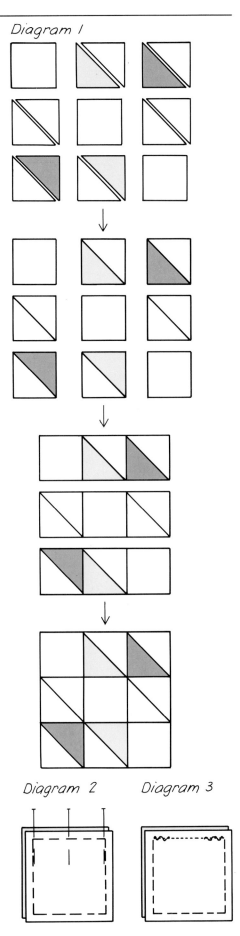

Diagram 1

Diagram 2   Diagram 3

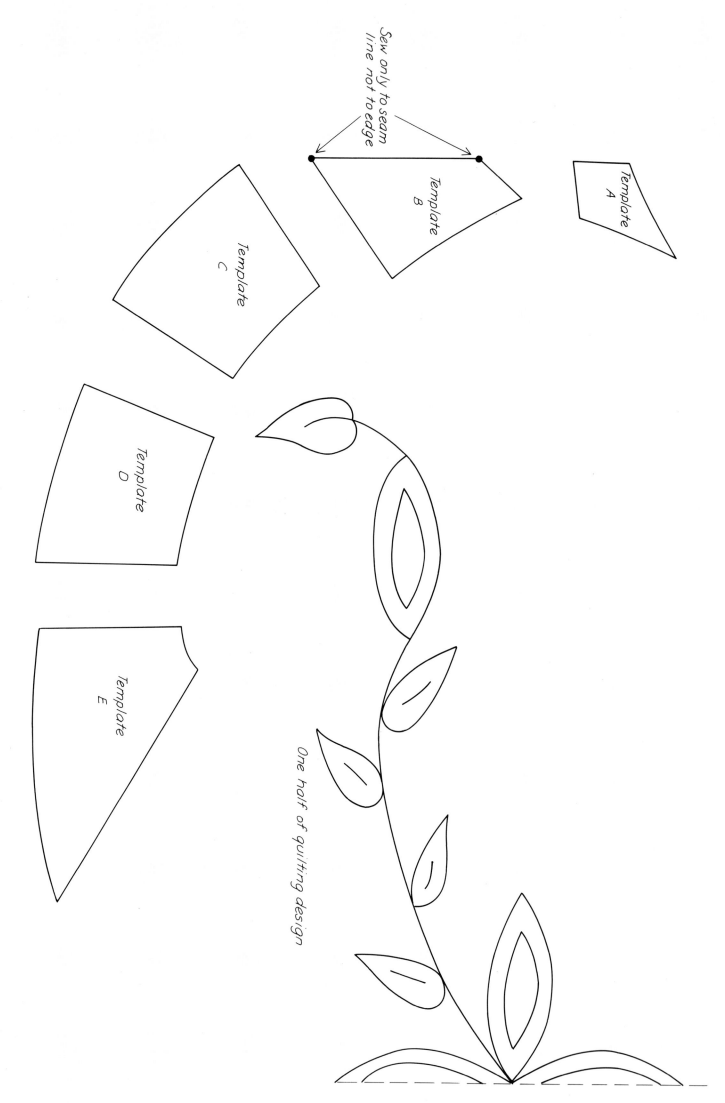

Template
A

Template
B

Sew only to seam
line not to edge

Template
C

Template
D

Template
E

One half of quilting design

Wedding Ring Bouquet
Hand-Pieced Cushion

Adapted from Aunt Martha's Creations.
Finished size: 16 × 16 inches (405 × 405 millimetres)

MATERIALS

Small quantities of assorted cotton prints for the patches
For cushion front: background fabric, batting and lining fabric, each 20 inches (510 millimetres) square
For cushion back: two pieces, each 17 × 11 inches (430 × 280 millimetres)
Piping: 70 inches (1.8 metres) piping cord
        70 inches (1.8 metres) of 2 inch (50 millimetre) bias strip, folded in two, to cover piping cord
Velcro: 16 inches (405 millimetres)
For cushion insert: Two pieces of fabric, each 18 inches (460 millimetres) square
Cushion filling: polyester or wool

Diagram 4

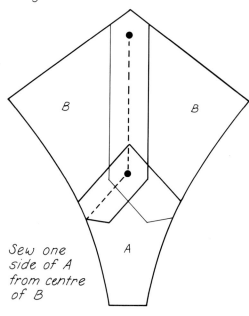

Sew one
side of A
from centre
of B

Diagram 5

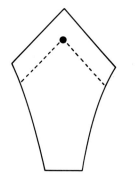

Diagram 6

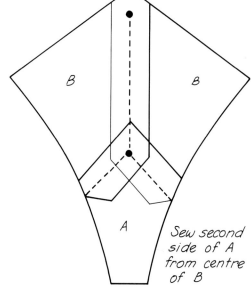

A

Sew second
side of A
from centre
of B

METHOD

MAKE TEMPLATES, using the patterns provided here, adding a ¼ inch (6 millimetre) seam allowance.

Cut four pieces in shapes A, B, C, D and E. Cut another four pieces each of B, C, D and E with the template reversed.

HAND PIECE C, D and E as they are shown in the template layout, sewing from edge to edge. Join B to C, sewing only to the seam line on the outer edge, as this makes it easier to turn in the ¼ inch (6 millimetre) seam when appliqueing the pieced work to the background. To inset piece A, pin the centre point of A to B and sew the short side, swing piece A round to sew second side (see diagrams 4–6).

Repeat until all four petals are sewn.

Lightly press diagonal creases in the background fabric, position the petals over the crease lines, being careful to centre the four A pieces in the middle point of the fabric. Pin and tack securely. HAND APPLIQUE the patches to the background fabric.

MARK THE QUILTING DESIGN.

Place the pieced cushion front over the batting and lining. Pin, then baste the layers together securely.

Put the work into a quilting hoop and HAND QUILT.

Pipe and COMPLETE THE CUSHION.

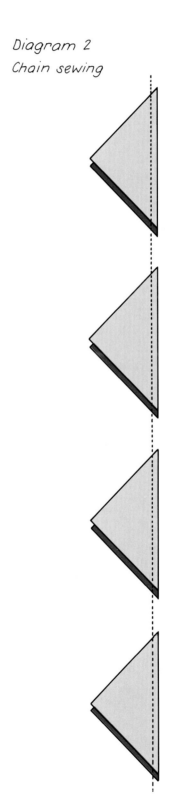

Diagram 1
To butt seam allowances
sewing direction

Diagram 2
Chain sewing

Machine piecing is the quickest and strongest method of sewing the shapes together and makes it possible to use heavier fabrics such as corduroy or woollens, both of which would be difficult to hand sew. Shapes smaller than 1½ inches (40 millimetres) are not suitable for machine piecing. Machine piecing requires a precise cutting line exactly ¼ inch (6 millimetres) from the sewing line because the sewing machine presser foot is aligned with the cut edge of the fabric, and the seam line need not be marked on the fabric.

Use a template that includes a ¼ inch (6 millimetre) seam allowance. Place the template face down on the wrong side of the fabric and draw around it. Cut out along the marked line.

Check that your sewing machine sews an exact ¼ inch (6 millimetre) seam when the edge of the presser foot is aligned with the edge of the fabric. If not, place a strip of masking tape on the foot plate of the machine so that it can be used as a guide for an accurate seam, or use a magnetic seam guide.

Lay out the pieces and plan a joining sequence. Place the first two pieces to be joined right sides together and sew from edge to edge. Guide the edge of the fabric along the edge of the presser foot (or the masking tape strip). Your sewing will be more accurate if you watch the presser foot position rather than the needle position. It is not necessary to backstitch at the beginning or end of a seam that will be crossed by another seam.

Where seamlines meet, pin accurately by inserting the pin into the seamlines at right angles to the line to be sewn. Sew right up to the pin and sew carefully over it, so that the pieces are held firmly and do not move while the stitching is done. Where possible, turn the seam allowances to opposite sides—the upper seam allowance towards the needle and the lower one away from the needle. The machine will then butt the shoulder of one seam against the other so that seam lines will meet exactly (diagram 1).

FAST AND ACCURATE MACHINE-PIECING TECHNIQUES

Chain sewing
This is an efficient method of machine piecing that is particularly useful when joining many identical units, such as a series of triangles that are all joined into squares, which are then made up into the block design. Simply feed the pairs of triangles, right sides together, through the sewing machine assembly-line fashion. Do not clip the threads between each pair of triangles—keep sewing until all units have been joined, forming a long chain. Then cut the units apart, press and repeat the process to join the larger units until the block is complete (diagram 2).

Cutting corners
This technique is used to produce templates for machine piecing that

Diagram 3

If your piecing looks
more like this

than this

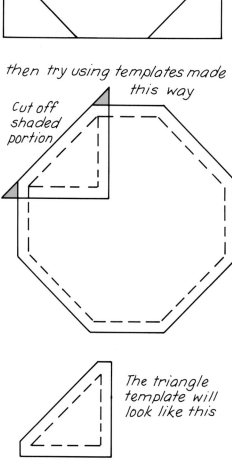

then try using templates made
this way

Cut off
shaded
portion

The triangle
template will
look like this

allow the edges to be aligned exactly. Once you have mastered it, you will be saved from frustration and inaccuracy.

Problems arise with machine piecing because a seam allowance is added to the shape and the cut edge is the sewing guide, but when angles are smaller than a right angle, the seam allowance projects by varying amounts beyond the seam line, depending on the size of the angle. Then when different shapes must be joined, if you align their cut edges when you are beginning to sew, the seam will be hopelessly inaccurate (diagram 3). This difficulty can be avoided by modifying the templates. Add the required seam allowance and cut the templates using template plastic. Then lay one template over another in the way the patches will be joined. Align the seams, then trim off the points extending beyond the other template. It sounds complicated, but by studying the diagrams you will see how it is done. The same shape will not always be trimmed in the same way, it depends how it is to be joined to other pieces. When the patches are cut using templates modified in this manner, the edges can be aligned exactly when each seam is sewn and the results will be accurate.

Caesar's Crown Variation Machine-Pieced Cushion

Finished size: 14½ inches (370 millimetres) diameter

MATERIALS

Small quantities of assorted cotton prints, in co-ordinating colours for the patches

For cushion front: lining fabric and batting, each 18 inches (460 millimetres) square

For cushion back: piece of any of the front fabrics 18 inches (460 millimetres) square

Piping: 50 inches (1.27 metres) piping cord
       50 inches (1.27 metres) of 2 inch (50 millimetre) bias strip, folded in two, to cover piping cord

Cushion filling: polyester or wool

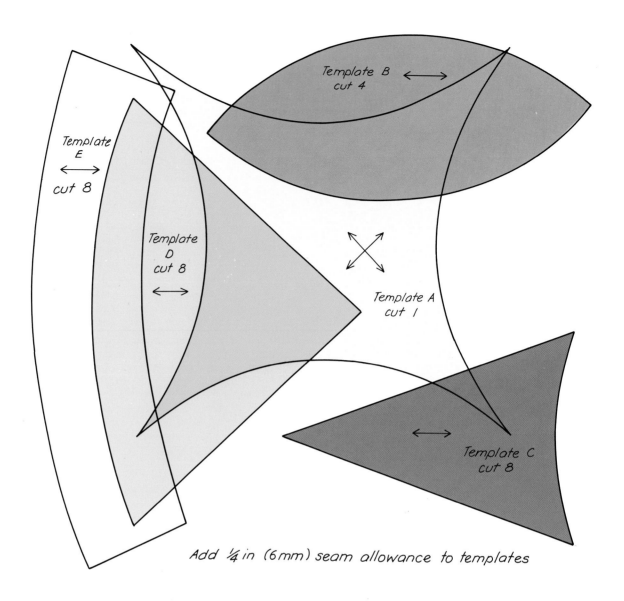

Template B
cut 4

Template
E

cut 8

Template
D
cut 8

Template A
cut 1

Template C
cut 8

Add ¼ in (6mm) seam allowance to templates

Placement guide

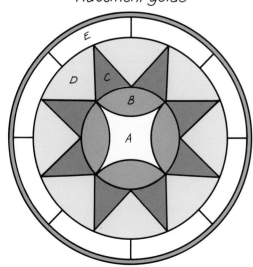

METHOD

MAKE TEMPLATES adding ¼ inch (6 millimetre) seam allowance.

Cut out all pattern pieces.

Join the four B pieces to centre piece A, to make unit 1.

Join all the C and D pieces, following the placement diagram, to make unit 2.

Join all the E pieces, to make unit 3.

Join units 1, 2 and 3, following the placement diagram. This stage may be completed by hand or by machine.

Place the pieced cushion front over the batting and lining. Pin, then baste the layers together securely. Put the work into a quilting hoop and HAND QUILT close to the seam lines around all the pieces.

Sew the covered piping round the cushion front and tack the back piece of the cushion over the front and sew together, being careful to sew just inside the piping stitching. Leave an opening of 6 inches (150 millimetres) for filling. Fill with polyester or wool and slipstitch the opening together.

"English" piecing is a hand-sewing technique that produces very accurate results and is especially suitable for difficult designs that require pieces to be inset. The patches are basted to paper patterns, producing accurate, finished size pieces, which are then whipstitched together. When the pieces have been joined, the papers are removed.

Make accurate templates from plastic or cardboard, with no seam allowance.

Use the templates to cut patterns out of paper or lightweight card. The paper must be firm enough to hold its shape, but not so firm that it is difficult to push a needle through it.

On the wrong side of the papers, mark any edges that will be on the outer edge of the block because these edges will not need to be turned under.

Pin the papers right side down on the wrong side of the fabric. Cut out, adding ¼ inch (6 millimetre) seam allowance, which can be judged by eye (diagram 1).

Fold the seam allowance to the wrong side, over the paper, and baste. Make sure that the fabric is folded exactly against the edge of the paper and that the corners are neat and accurate. Knot the end of a length of thread and begin and end the stitching on the right side, so that the basting threads can easily be removed when the piecing is completed. Do not turn under the seam allowance on the marked edges (diagram 2).

Press the basted patches lightly. Lay them out in their correct position. Pick up two adjoining patches, hold them right sides together, and sew together. Use a whipstitch and a thread that matches the darker fabric. Secure the stitching at each end of the seam. Be careful to stitch through the folded edge of the fabric only, not through the paper (diagram 3).

When all the patches have been joined, press lightly. Remove the basting threads and the paper patterns.

Diagram 1

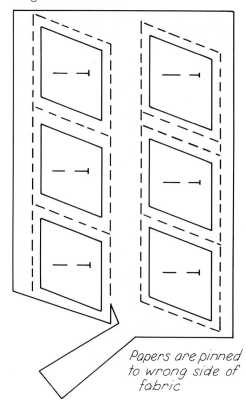

Papers are pinned to wrong side of fabric

Diagram 2

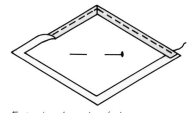

Fabric basted to paper

Diagram 3

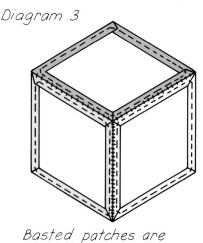

Basted patches are whipstitched together

Broken Star
English-Pieced Cushion

Finished size: 16 × 16 inches (405 × 405 millimetres)

MATERIALS

27 inches (685 millimetres) solid green fabric (includes backing)
9 inches (230 millimetres) rust coloured floral
9 inches (230 millimetres) apricot pin-dot design
Scraps of green pin-dot or green small floral design
Scraps of rust-coloured chintz
Batting and lining fabric, each 18 inches (460 millimetres) square
Piping: 70 inches (1.8 metres) of piping cord
       70 inches (1.8 metres) of 2 inch (50 millimetre) bias strip,
       folded in two, to cover piping cord
Velcro: 16 inches (405 millimetres)
For cushion back: two pieces, each 17 × 11 inches (430 × 280 millimetres)
These pieces are cut from the solid green fabric.
For cushion insert: two pieces of fabric, each 18 inches (460 millimetres)
square
Cushion filling: polyester or wool

METHOD

Cut the following patches:
4 pieces of A in the apricot pin-dot design
24 pieces of B in the apricot pin-dot design
32 pieces of B in the rust-coloured floral
20 pieces of B in the rust-coloured chintz
36 pieces of B in the solid green
8 pieces of B in the green pin-dot or green small floral

Prepare the patches for ENGLISH PIECING.

Trace the quilting diagram and colour it in according to the colours of your chosen fabrics. This makes arranging and sewing the patches much easier.

Join the patches in eight rows across, then sew the rows together, carefully matching the seams.

Remove the papers and press lightly.

Lay the completed cushion front over the batting and lining. Baste the layers together securely. HAND QUILT ¼ inch (6 millimetres) from the seam lines as suggested in the quilting diagram.

COMPLETE THE CUSHION.

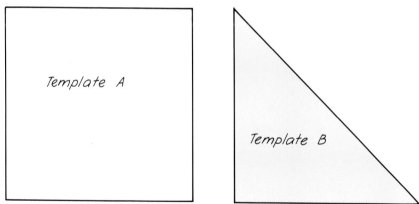

Add ¼ in (6mm) seam allowance when cutting fabric

Quilting diagram

Applique means applying one fabric to another in a chosen design. The design may be freely drawn and cut, or a more formal pattern may be used. Traditionally the designs were quite simple and child-like but some of the appliqued works being produced today are works of art and complicated in design. Firm, non-fraying fabrics are best suited to hand applique but a variety of textures and trims can be used to create an interesting effect.

Place the applique pattern face up on the right side of the fabric.

Draw around the pattern in pencil.

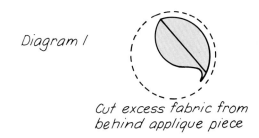

Diagram 1

Cut out, allowing ¼ inch (6 millimetre) seam allowance. Try to place the patterns so that the grain of the fabric is running the same way throughout the block, especially with the larger pieces.

Cut excess fabric from behind applique piece

To baste, turn the seam allowance to the wrong side so that the pencil line is no longer visible and baste the edge in place with running stitches. Use a contrasting thread and begin and end the stitching on the right side of the fabric so that the basting stitches will be easy to remove. Do not turn under or baste any edges that will be overlapped by other pieces.

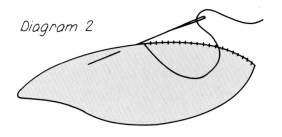

Diagram 2

Lightly press the basted pieces.

When all the pieces have been basted and pressed, prepare the background fabric. Lightly trace the design onto the background fabric.

Position the applique pieces on the background fabric. Secure the pieces by basting them in place or by placing small pieces of fusible webbing between the pieces and the background and ironing to fuse them.

Stitch the patches in place by working from the background forward. That is, sew the patches that are behind others in place first, then add other layers. It is a good idea to cut away the background fabric from beneath the patches (very carefully!) as you work, to avoid the build up of several layers of fabric, which would be bulky and would make quilting very difficult (diagram 1).

Stitch the patches in place with an 18 inch (500 millimetre) length of thread that matches the colour of the patch, not the background colour. If the patch has several contrasting colours, it is better to choose a neutral beige or grey that will be inconspicuous on all the colours in the fabric, rather than match, for example, the red of a red, white and blue print, and have it stand out on the blue and white areas.

The stitch used in applique is a blind stitch, which shows just a tiny spot of thread on the front and a slightly longer (1/8 inch or 3 millimetres) length of thread on the back. Bring the thread up through the background fabric and catch just a couple of threads on the fold of the applique patch. Push the needle down through the background right above the spot where it came up, and move the needle about 1/8 inch (3 millimetres) away to come up through the background and patch again (diagram 2). Pull the stitches firmly but not too tightly. Make all beginning and ending

Diagram 3

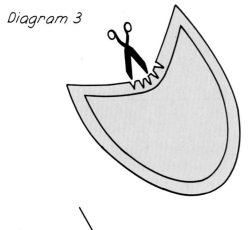

Diagram 4

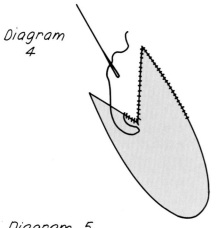

Diagram 5

Diagram 6

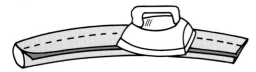

Diagram 7

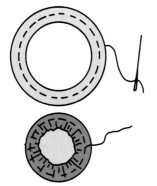

knots or backstitches on the back, and weave the loose thread ends into the seam allowances on the back so they will not show through the background fabric later.

When the applique work is finished, remove the basting threads carefully, and clip away any excess background fabric from underneath. Press gently – applique work should not be ironed absolutely flat.

HINTS

Concave curves
Use a pair of very sharp embroidery scissors to clip into the seam allowance almost to the seam line. When appliqueing, it will be necessary to stitch more closely on the concave curves (diagrams 3 and 4).

Points
Trim the seam allowance across the point, then fold it under. Turn under the seam allowance approaching the point and stitch as far as the point. Then turn under the seam allowance on the other side of the point, take a few extra stitches at the point, and continue stitching away from the point (diagram 5).

Narrow strips—straight or curved
Cut bias strips of the fabric twice the desired width, plus ¼ inch (6 millimetres). Fold the strips in half lengthways, *wrong sides together*, and sew with an 1/8 inch (3 millimetre) seam. Fold the seam allowances to one side, and press so that the seam allowances and the stitching line are on the underside (diagram 6). Cut the strips to the required length. When appliqueing the strip in place as a curved piece, stitch the concave curves first, then stitch the outer curves.

Circles
To make a perfect circle, cut a thin cardboard circle of the desired size, and cut fabric circles with ¼ inch (6 millimetre) seam allowance added. Sew a running stitch around the circle within the seam allowance and place the cardboard circle in the centre of the wrong side of the fabric. Pull the thread ends of the running stitch to gather the fabric up over the cardboard. Press, remove the cardboard circle, and press again (diagram 7).

OTHER METHODS OF HAND APPLIQUE

Direct applique

Cut out the pieces as above, but with a reduced seam allowance – about 1/8 inch (3 millimetres). Position the patches without turning under the seam allowances and baste in place on the background fabric. Turn under a section of the seam allowance and finger press. Begin stitching as above, and use the point of the needle to turn the seam allowance under as stitching proceeds.

Starch and template applique

For each different pattern piece, cut a template from light-weight cardboard. Place the template on the fabric and cut out with a ¼ inch (6 millimetre) seam allowance. Place the fabric, right side down, on the ironing board. Place the cardboard template on top of the fabric. Spray with spray-on starch and turn the seam allowances over the template. Press, easing in fullness or clipping where necessary. Remove the template and press again. The pattern piece is now ready to baste in place on the background fabric.

Freezer paper applique

This has become a very popular technique in the United States. If freezer paper is available where you live, the *Quilter's Newsletter Magazine* of April 1987, number 191, page 30, explains this technique. The magazine is produced by Leman Publications Inc., 6700 West 44th Avenue, Wheatridge, Colorado, USA 80033.

Floral Bouquet
Hand-Applique Cushion

Finished size: 16 × 16 inches (405 × 405 millimetres)

MATERIALS

Small quantities of assorted cotton prints
For cushion front: background fabric, batting, and lining fabric, each
20 inches (510 millimetres) square
For cushion back: two pieces each 17 × 11 inches (430 × 280 millimetres)
Binding: 70 inches (1.8 metres) of 1¼ inch (30 millimetre) bias strip
Velcro strip: 16 inches (405 millimetres)
For cushion insert: two pieces of fabric, each 18 inches (460 millimetres)
square
Cushion filling: polyester or wool

METHOD

On a large sheet of tracing paper, draw a 16 inch (405 millimetre) square. Mark horizontal and vertical centre lines. Trace the pattern for the bouquet, matching the centre lines. Use a felt pen so that the design can be easily traced onto the fabric.

Tape the pattern onto LIGHT BOX. Press light horizontal and vertical centre creases in background fabric. Lay the fabric over the pattern, matching the creases to the centre lines. Lightly trace the design onto the fabric.

Using the light box, trace each pattern piece onto the appropriate fabric, making a fine pencil line on the right side of the fabric. Use a dotted line for edges that will be overlapped by other pieces. Cut out all the pieces, adding ¼ inch (6 millimetre) seam allowance.

HAND APPLIQUE the pieces in place. Use ¼ inch (6 millimetre) bias strips for all stems. Press lightly. Embroider the stamens, leaf veins and so on if desired.

Mark the ripple quilting design as shown in the photograph of the cushion, using a fine pencil line.

Place the cushion front over the batting and lining squares. Pin the layers together and baste carefully, making sure that the layers remain smooth. Note that the cushion front is larger than the finished size—it will be cut down to a 16½ inch (420 millimetre) square when the quilting is finished, but the larger working piece is recommended because the quilting tends to "shrink" the work, and because a larger piece often fits more easily into a quilting hoop.

Place the work in a quilting hoop or square frame, HAND QUILT along ripple lines and around each applique piece—stitch in the background fabric but very close to the applique piece. When the quilting is completed, mark a 17 inch (430 millimetre) square, centred over the design and cut the cushion front down to this size.

COMPLETE THE CUSHION, using a bound edge.

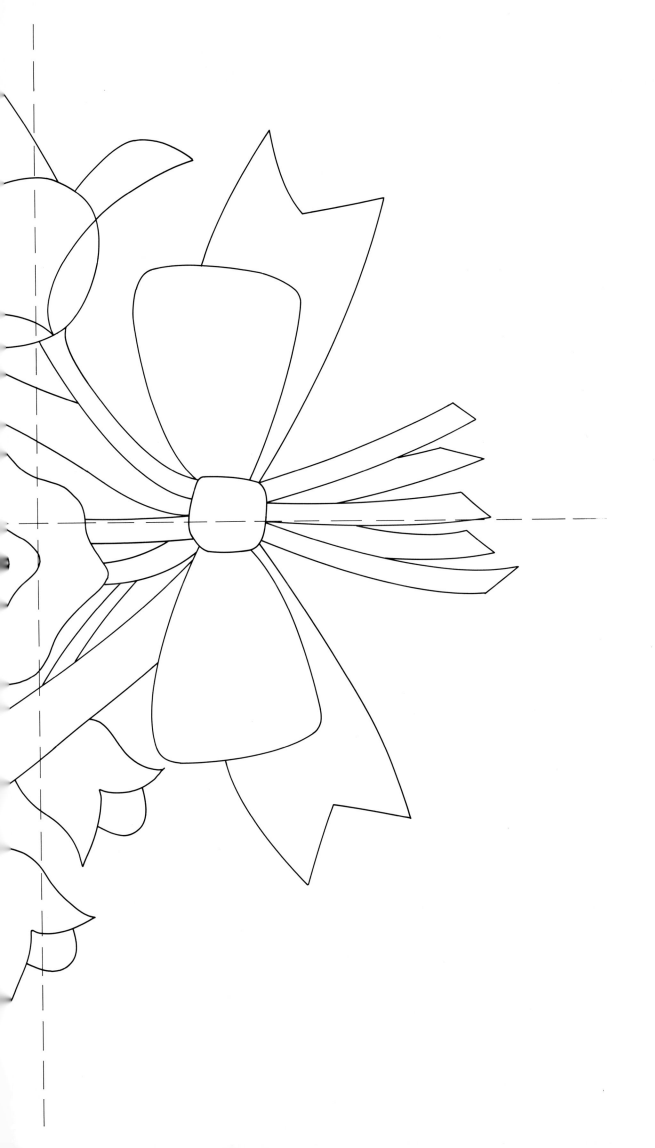

21

Ripple Quilting Pattern
Trace, joining sections. Glue onto cardboard, and cut out a template.

Machine applique is an alternative to hand applique that permits the use of heavier materials, as it is not necessary to turn under a hem which could show as a bulky ridge. Inspiration for designs can come from many sources, children's colouring books, photographs, pictures and everyday objects.

Lay a piece of iron-on interfacing over the pattern (reversed) and trace each piece. Iron the interfacing onto the wrong side of the fabric and cut out the fabric and interfacing along the marked line. The interfacing is used to stabilize the fabric and reduce fraying. Add ¼ inch (6 millimetre) seam allowance on edges overlapped by other pieces.

Place the background fabric over the design and lightly mark sufficient lines to guide the placement of the pattern pieces.

Place the pattern pieces on the background fabric. Slip a piece of fusible webbing under each piece and iron. The fusible webbing will hold the pieces in place while the applique stitching is done. Alternatively, the pieces can be basted in place or held with magic tape. It is very important that the pieces are secured because the stitching will not proceed easily if the pieces are not held firmly in place. Whichever method is used to hold the pieces, leave the edges free, so that if a piece is overlapped by another, the top piece can be lifted aside and the applique stitching begun beneath the upper piece. When the upper piece is stitched, the start of the sewing on the lower piece will be covered and secured.

Before beginning the applique, it is imperative to experiment on a trial piece, using the same fabric as you will use for the project. The sewing machine must be adjusted to produce the most attractive stitch possible, as it is a feature of the finished item. Practice is also necessary in order to achieve a smooth and professional finish. Consult the instruction book of your sewing machine for suggestions about satin stitch or applique. Some machines have a bobbin case with an extra hole through which the bobbin thread is passed when doing satin stitch. It has the effect of increasing the lower thread tension so that the upper thread is drawn slightly to the lower side of the fabric and the lower thread is not visible at all on the right side of the fabric. This produces a very attractive satin stitch. The success of machine applique depends very much on the quality of the machine stitching so take the time to clean and oil the machine and fit a new needle. If you have difficulty obtaining a good satin stitch, consult your sewing machine dealer, who may be able to suggest ways of improving the stitch quality. Some machines have an open embroidery foot, which is most helpful for satin stitch because it allows you to see the stitching much more easily. Set the machine to satin stitch and begin stitching a practice piece. Adjust the length and width of the stitch until it is close and even. On its right hand swing, the needle should go into the background fabric immediately beside the applique fabric. Most of the stitch should be over the applique fabric to prevent fraying. Sew slowly but steadily. Avoid unnecessary stops and starts and keep the stitching line smooth. When turning a corner, stitch right up to the corner and

Diagram 1

Zigzag stitch

Applique stitch

stop with the needle in the fabric on its right hand swing. Turn the fabric and begin stitching. The first few stitches will cover the previous stitching.

When ready to start stitching the pattern pieces, begin with those that are partly beneath others. Where possible, start stitching beneath the upper piece, so that the start of stitching will be overlapped and secured. When stitching upper pieces, the thread ends must be pulled to the wrong side of the fabric and knotted, otherwise the satin stitch will soon unravel.

The stitching is done in two stages. First, sew around the edges with an open zigzag stitch to secure the piece. Then change to satin stitch and stitch again (diagram 1). To prevent puckering, place a sheet of paper (typing weight) under the fabric while sewing. When the sewing is complete, tear the paper away.

It is usual to choose a thread colour that matches the applique piece. However, if you wish to make the outline of the pieces a prominent part of the design, choose a contrasting thread colour.

Iowa Rose Wreath
Machine-Applique Cushion

Finished size: 16 × 16 inches (405 × 405 millimetres)

MATERIALS

Small quantities of assorted cotton prints
For cushion front: fabric, batting and lining, each 20 inches (510 millimetres) square
For cushion back: two pieces, each 17 × 11 inches (430 × 280 millimetres)
Piping: 70 inches (1.8 metres)
Velcro: 16 inches (405 millimetres)
For cushion insert: two pieces of fabric, each 18 inches (460 millimetres) square
Cushion filling: polyester or wool

Diagram 1
Placement guide

METHOD

On a large sheet of tracing paper, draw a 17 inch (430 millimetre) square. Mark diagonal lines from corner to corner of the square. Trace the pattern into each quarter of the square in the same position. Use a felt pen to give a bold outline. The base of the stem should be ¾ inch (20 millimetres) from the diagonal line, and the lines should pass through the rose as shown in diagram 1.

Press light diagonal creases in the background fabric and place it over the pattern on a LIGHT BOX, matching the creases to the diagonal lines. Lightly trace the design onto the fabric.

Cut out all the pattern pieces, position them on the background fabric and MACHINE APPLIQUE.

Mark quilting lines on the creased lines. The rest of the quilting lines will be marked parallel to these with 1 inch (25 millimetre) masking tape.

Place the cushion front over the batting and lining. Pin, then baste the layers together securely. Put the work into a quilting hoop or square frame. HAND QUILT the background in a cross-hatch design (see photograph).

COMPLETE THE CUSHION.

Iowa Rose Wreath

Hand quilting, like so many needlework techniques, is centuries old. It originally had the very practical purpose of joining together several layers of material to create warmth. The quilting designs may be the only decoration on the project, or it may be used to enhance patchwork or applique.

Mark the quilting design of your choice on the fabric using a fine pencil line. Baste the top, batting and lining together, and put into a quilting hoop.

Thread a quilting needle with a 20 inch (500 millimetre) length of thread and knot the end. Quilting thread is strong and resists tangling, but if it is unobtainable, or not available in a particular colour, machine thread can be used successfully, especially if the thread is run over a piece of beeswax before use.

Wear a thimble on the middle finger of the right hand (if right-handed). If you are not used to using a thimble, persevere—it will soon become perfectly comfortable and you will be able to quilt quickly and without damage to your fingers. Some quilters also wear a thimble on the index finger of the other hand, which is beneath the work and has the job of feeling the point of the needle as it is pushed through the fabric, and directing the needle back to the top of the quilt. Others find a thimble on this finger clumsy and can manage without, usually by using the side of the fingernail rather than the surface of the finger. Other suggestions are to paint the skin surface with nail varnish, or to put tape on the finger. It requires experimentation until you find a method which is comfortable for you.

The quilting stitch is a simple running stitch. The stitches should be small, evenly spaced and straight. Stitches will become smaller with practice, but to begin with concentrate on making the stitches uniform in size and straight. Try to make the length of the space between the stitches equal to the length of the stitches.

Begin quilting by inserting the needle into the top of the quilt about 1 inch (25 millimetres) away from the starting point of the quilting line. Bring the needle up at the starting point and tug gently on the thread so that the knot is pulled through the fabric and is buried in the batting.

Insert the needle into the fabric close to where it came up and push the needle to the underside using the thimble. With the index finger of the hand under the work, feel the tip of the needle and direct the needle back to the top. With a rocking motion, repeat the process so that there are two or three stitches on the needle, then push the needle through the fabric with the thimble, grasp the needle and pull the thread through the work. Repeat this process. You may prefer to take just one stitch at a time to begin with, but you will find that it is much faster to take several stitches before pulling the thread through.

Types of Quilting Design

Diagram 1
Outline

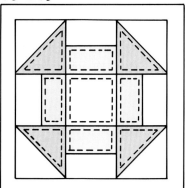

Diagram 2
Outline

Diagram 3
Ornamental motif

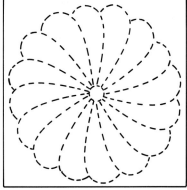

Diagram 4
Allover quilting

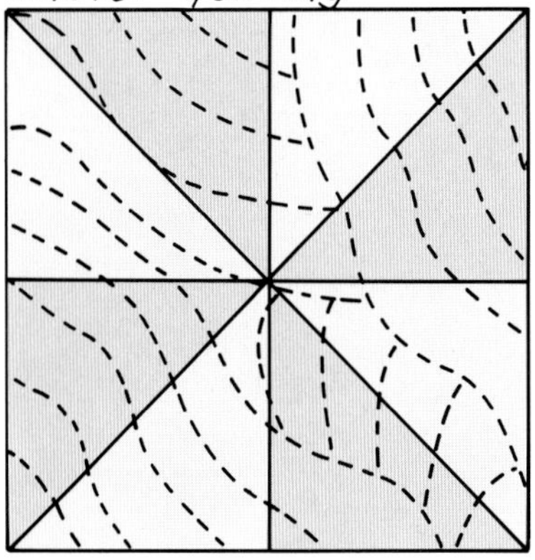

End a line of stitching by knotting the thread before taking the last stitch. Run the needle under the surface after the last stitch, bring it to the top and tug the knot into the batting. Cut the thread close to the surface of the fabric and the thread end will disappear into the quilt. Alternatively, if the quilting ends near a seam, you can run the needle beneath the surface from the last stitch to the seam line. Bring the needle up in the seam line, take a tiny backstitch, then run the needle along the seam line, beneath the surface for a short distance. Bring the needle to the surface again and clip the thread. When quilting a cushion top, the underside will not be seen, so the stitching can be begun and ended neatly on the underside. But on a quilt the stitching should be neat on both sides and there should be no visible evidence of where a row of stitching started or finished. Avoid unnecessary stops and starts by planning the direction of stitching. When a motif has been completed, it is often possible to run the needle under the surface of the fabric to the next motif and continue stitching without starting afresh.

TYPES OF QUILTING DESIGN

Outline quilting
This is the most traditional and most frequently used method. Each piece in the quilt top is quilted ¼ inch (6 millimetres) in from the seam line. Alternatively, a particular shape in the design may be outlined, instead of each piece (diagrams 1 and 2).

Motif quilting
Elaborate motifs are often quilted in areas of the quilt that are not pieced. In wholecloth work, the entire design is quilted onto a plain fabric — there is no piecing (diagram 3).

Background quilting
An allover design is often quilted in the background. Examples are shown in diagrams 6–9.

Allover quilting
A quilting design may be stitched over the entire surface of the quilt, without regard to the pattern formed by the pieces that make up the quilt. The design may reflect the lines of the piecing, or it may be totally different. For example, an angular pieced design may have a quilting design of flowing curves superimposed (diagram 4).

MARKING THE QUILTING DESIGN ON THE FABRIC

There are several ways of transferring the design to the fabric and your choice of method depends on the colour and type of fabric, the nature of the design and your personal preference. It is best to be versatile, as no one method will be suitable for all situations. Experiment with the following techniques.

Tracing

Draw the design onto tracing paper with felt pen so that the outline is bold and easily seen. Lay the fabric over the design and pin or tape it in place. Trace the design onto the fabric using a fine soft-leaded pencil or dressmaking pencil. Use a LIGHT BOX if necessary. Water-erasable pens can be used, but as the long-term effects of the chemicals in the pen on the fabric are not yet known, and some quilters have had difficulty removing the pen marks, we do not recommend their use, especially on a potential heirloom. Some antique quilts have pencil lines still faintly visible, but the pencil has not damaged the fabric. Tracing is a suitable method for curved and intricate designs. Tracing must be done before the layers are basted together.

Stencil

Trace the design onto a piece of template plastic, or draw it on card, and cut it out. Place the stencil on the fabric, tape in place and draw around the stencil. This method can be used before or after the layers are basted together. It is suitable for use when a design is repeatedly used and has the advantage that the design can be marked as required, which is less tedious than doing all the marking at once, as must be done when the design is traced before assembling the layers.

Masking tape

This is an excellent method for straight-line designs, outline quilting and cross-hatching. For outline quilting, use ¼ inch (6 millimetre) masking tape. Place a strip of masking tape on the quilt, with the edge aligned with the seam line. Stitch along the opposite edge of the tape. After each line is stitched, the tape can be removed and reused until it no longer adheres closely. Wider masking tape is useful for parallel lines and cross-hatching. It may be necessary to mark the first line with ruler and pencil, but tape of the appropriate width can be used for subsequent lines parallel to the first line. Although adhesive substances can damage or stain fabric, I have used masking tape repeatedly for a number of years without ever having any adverse effect. It is important, however, to remove the tape as soon as stitching is finished and not leave it on the fabric when not quilting. The advantage of this method is that it does not involve marking the fabric at all, and by using masking tape of the required width, measuring can be avoided. Masking tape is also useful for removing stray threads, dust and fluff from the surface of the finished quilt: simply glide a length of tape over the surface, holding the ends taut and the sticky surface will pick up the threads.

Unmarked quilting

Experienced quilters develop a very accurate eye and you may find that you are able to outline quilt satisfactorily without any marking.

Types of Quilting Design

Diagram 6
Shell

Diagram 7
Echo

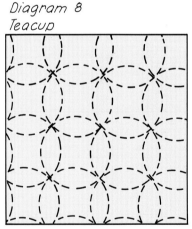

Diagram 8
Teacup

Diagram 9
Diamond cross-hatch

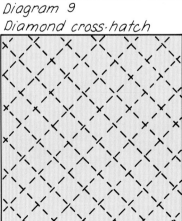

Hand-Quilted Cushion

Finished size: 16 × 16 inches (405 × 405 millimetres)

MATERIALS

For cushion front: fabric, batting and lining, each 20 inches (510 millimetres) square
For cushion back: 2 pieces, each 17 × 11 inches (430 × 280 millimetres)
Piping: 70 inches (1.8 metres)
Velcro strip: 16 inches (405 millimetres)
For cushion insert: two pieces of fabric, each 18 inches (460 millimetres) square
Cushion filling: polyester or wool

METHOD

On a large sheet of tracing paper, draw a 16 inch (405 millimetre) square. Mark horizontal and vertical centre lines. Trace the pattern, matching the centre lines. Use a felt pen so that the design can be easily traced onto the fabric.

Tape the pattern onto a LIGHT BOX. Lightly press horizontal and vertical centre creases in fabric. Lay the fabric over the pattern, matching the creases to the centre lines. Lightly trace the design onto the fabric.

Lay the fabric over the batting and lining and align the edges. Pin the layers together and baste securely. Put into a quilting hoop or square frame.

HAND QUILT the design on the marked lines.

When the quilting is completed, mark a 17 inch (430 millimetre) square on the fabric, centred over the design. Baste just inside the marked line and cut down to size.

COMPLETE THE CUSHION.

Many quilters believe that machine quilting is quick, easy and second-rate. It is certainly faster than hand quilting, but top-quality machine quilting requires considerable skill, and the result can be marvellous. It is ideal for items that are likely to receive considerable wear and frequent washing, such as clothing, bags, soft furnishings and baby quilts. Machine quilting is not such a relaxing or sociable pastime as hand quilting is, but it may be the most suitable method, depending on the intended use of the item and the time available to the quilter. The technique does require practice, a sewing machine that will co-operate and, for large items, a spacious and well organized work area. Consult your sewing machine dealer for advice—there may be accessories available, such as a walking foot, which will help you to get best results.

Make up a trial square of fabric, batting and lining. Baste the layers together. Experiment with stitches, tension, single or twin needles, and stitch length. Where possible, begin and end the stitching at the edge of the fabric where the stitch can be secured by backstitching that will not be visible in the finished item. If you need to start or finish in the middle of the work, the thread ends must be pulled to the underside and secured, so the quilting does not unravel. Machine quilting can be successful in areas where hand quilting is difficult, such as over bulky seams, and it can also be used on heavy-weight fabrics that would not be suitable for hand quilting. It is most important to baste the layers very securely so they do not pucker while being fed through the machine. Use a thin batting, such as needlepunch, for the best results. Machine quilting is most successful when the item is very closely quilted, so that the three layers become one textile. For examples of this, see the quilts by Malcolm Harrison in the Gallery section of this book.

Machine-Quilted Cushion

Finished size: 16 × 16 inches (405 × 405 millimetres)

MATERIALS

For cushion front: chintz, batting and lining, each 20 inches (510 millimetres) square

For cushion back: two pieces, each 17 × 11 inches (430 × 280 millimetres)

Piping: 70 inches (1.8 metres)

Velcro: 16 inches (405 millimetres)

For cushion insert: two pieces of fabric, each 18 inches (460 millimetres) square

Cushion filling: polyester or wool

METHOD

Mark a 17 inch (420 millimetre) square in the centre of the chintz fabric. Lightly mark a quilting design of your choice.

Place the chintz over the batting and lining and baste the layers together.

MACHINE QUILT along the marked lines, taking care not to allow the layers to become wrinkled. Secure all thread ends.

COMPLETE THE CUSHION.

Cathedral Window is a fascinating patchwork technique. Study the photograph of the cushion and you will see four designs emerge. The window, from which the name evolved, a circle surrounding the window, a four petalled flower where the circles intertwine and another small four-petalled flower at the centre of the large flower.

The Cathedral Window unit is made from two squares of fabric: the window fabric, usually calico or a solid colour, and the patch fabric, usually a print fabric.

Make cardboard templates of the desired size for the windows and the patches. Try 9 inch (230 millimetre) square window templates and 2½ inch (640 millimetre) square patch templates to begin with. These produce a unit of finished size 4 inches (100 millimetres).

Cut out the required number of window squares and patch squares. Fold the window squares in half, with the right sides together. Stitch across the ends with a ¼ inch (6 millimetre) seam (diagram 1), by hand or machine.

Open the rectangle and pin the seams together at the centre. Stitch across the opening with a ¼ inch (6 millimetre) seam, leaving a 1½ inch (40 millimetre) gap (diagram 2). Trim the corner points.

Turn right side out through the opening, press, and slipstitch the opening. Fold the corners of the square into the centre so that they meet, press. The crease lines will be the seam lines (diagram 3). Make the required number of these window units.

Place two window units seamless sides together, and stitch together along one crease line, backstitching at each end of the seam (diagram 4). Join sufficient window units to make a row of the desired width. Join the rows by placing them seamless sides together, carefully matching all the seams. Stitch along the crease line (diagram 5).

Fold the corners of the squares to the centre once more and tack the points together, securing them to the centre of the square.

Pin a patch square to each window square and baste in place. Turn the folded edges of the window squares forward to cover the raw edges of the patch square and blindstitch in place (diagram 6). Keep adding patches until they have all been stitched into position. To complete the petal design on the outer folded edges where no patches have been added, continue to fold and blindstitch these edges.

The Cathedral Window patchwork is now ready for use. It does not need lining or quilting. If desired, it may be attached to a background fabric that is larger than the Cathedral Window block so that it forms a border. The cushion instructions describe how to mount the block on a background.

Diagram 1

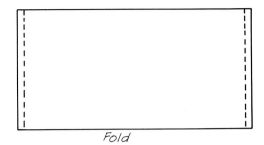

Fold

Diagram 2

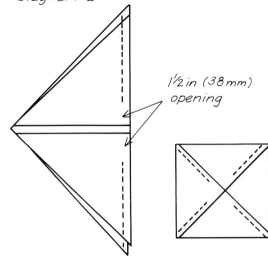

1½ in (38 mm)
opening

Diagram 3

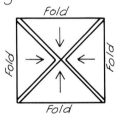

Fold
Fold
Fold
Fold

Completed window unit

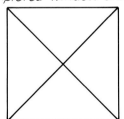

Diagram 4

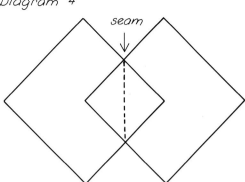

seam

Diagram 5

Stitching rows together

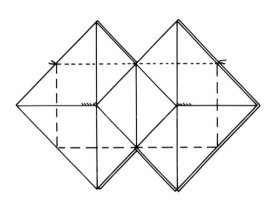

Diagram 6

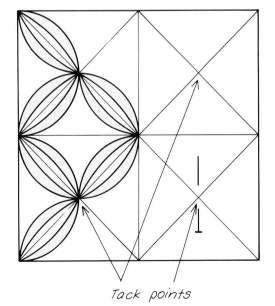

Tack points

Cathedral Window Cushion

This cushion reverses the conventional Cathedral Window method by making the windows out of the print fabric and using a solid colour for the background and window patches.

Finished size: 14½ × 14½ inches (370 × 370 millimetres)

MATERIALS

¾ yard (70 centimetres) background fabric for front, back and patches
½ yard (46 centimetres) printed fabric for windows
A scrap of light batting to pad the window patches (optional)
Covered piping cord 60 inches (1.52 metres)
Velcro: 14 inches (360 millimetres)
For cushion insert: two pieces of fabric 16 inches (410 millimetres) square
For cushion filling: polyester or wool

METHOD

Pre-wash fabrics and press.

For the windows, cut twelve 7 inch (180 millimetre) squares of the print fabric and twelve 2 inch (51 millimetre) squares of the background fabric for the window patches.

For the front, cut a 15 inch (380 millimetre) square of background fabric and lightly press in diagonal lines as a guide when positioning the cathedral block. Cut two pieces 12½ × 15 inches (320 × 380 millimetres) for the back.

Make the CATHEDRAL WINDOW block, referring to the photograph as a guide to the placement of the rows, and attach to the background as follows. Centre the block on the background using the pressed diagonal lines as a guide. With the flaps open along the outer edges of the block, stitch the block to the background along the crease lines (diagram 1). Fold the corners of the squares to the centre and tack in place.

The illustrated cushion had 1½ inch (40 millimetre) squares of light batting inserted behind the window patches. This makes them stand out nicely, but it is optional.

COMPLETE THE CUSHION.

Use this chart to determine the number of squares required and the amount of material for a particular cathedral window project.

Window square size	Finished window size	1 yard (1 metre) fabric yields	Window patch size
18 in (460 mm)	8½ in (220 mm)	4	5 in (130 mm)
11 in (280 mm)	5 in (130 mm)	12	3 in (76 mm)
10 in (250 mm)	4¾ in (120 mm)	12	2¾ in (70 mm)
9 in (230 mm)	4 in (100 mm)	20	2½ in (64 mm)
8 in (200 mm)	3¾ in (95 mm)	20	2¼ in (57 mm)
7 in (180 mm)	3¾ in (83 mm)	30	2 in (51 mm)
6 in (150 mm)	2¾ in (70 mm)	42	1½ in (38 mm)
5 in (130 mm)	2¼ in (57 mm)	63	1¼ in (32 mm)

Attaching Windows to Background

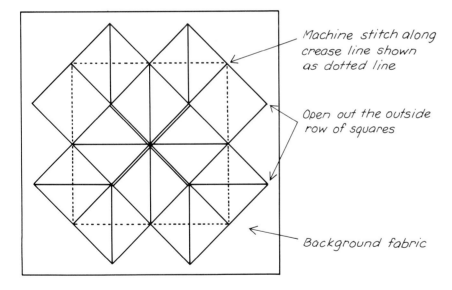

Machine stitch along crease line shown as dotted line

Open out the outside row of squares

Background fabric

Many designs can be constructed from two simple shapes—the square and the triangle. They can be easily pieced by machine so that a child can achieve quick results and at the same time learn how to design, cut and piece accurately.

All the patterns are based on a square block, which is divided into three or four units on each side, so that the square contains nine or sixteen small squares, some of which are divided into two right-angle triangles. Graph paper is used to draw up the designs and draft the patterns. Design possibilities are endless, and children may enjoy making their own design.

The Sailboat cushion was made by the 11-year-old son of one of the authors, and the Flower Basket is an example of another straightforward block that a young sewer could attempt. Do supervise young sewers closely, and teach them how to use the sewing machine, iron, scissors, rotary cutter and craft knife safely. Try to maintain a balance between encouraging them to achieve a satisfactory standard of work, by unpicking and re-sewing where necessary, and discouraging them by having unreasonably high expectations. It is important that children should produce something they can take pride in, but they should also feel enthusiastic about continuing and expanding their skills.

The following instructions describe the steps a child should follow to make the illustrated Sailboat cushion. The diagrams show a selection of designs, any of which could be made in the same manner. Use the half speed setting on your machine, if it has one.

If the child would like to tackle a larger project, twelve 12 inch (320 millimetre) blocks can be made into a quilt measuring 5 feet × 6 feet 3 inches (1.56 × 1.955 metres) using 3 inch (75 millimetre) sashing and 6 inch (150 millimetre) borders. The quilt could be TIED by the child, or possibly HAND QUILTED or MACHINE QUILTED by an adult volunteer (diagram 1).

METRIC MEASUREMENTS

The block size chosen should be one that will divide conveniently into four units on each side. A 12 inch block divides into four 3 inch units, but the exact metric equivalent, 305 millimetres, is not an easy measurement to work with. So in the following instructions, the metric measurements are based on a 320 millimetre block and are not exact equivalents and will not produce an identical size block. Therefore it is important to follow one set of measurements only.

Sailboat Cushion

Finished size: 16 × 16 inches (420 × 420 millimetres)

MATERIALS

Small quantities of cotton fabric in three colours
Needlepunch batting: 17 inch (445 millimetre) square
Lining fabric: 17 inch (445 millimetre) square
For cushion back: two pieces, each 17 × 11 inches (445 × 285 millimetres)
Velcro: 16 inches (360 millimetres)
For cushion insert: two pieces of fabric, each 18 inches (460 millimetres) square
Cushion filling: polyester or wool

METHOD

On a large sheet of graph paper draw a 12 inch (320 millimetre) square. Mark the 3 inch, 6 inch and 9 inch (80, 160, 240 millimetre) positions on each side, and rule lines connecting the marks, so that the square is divided into sixteen small squares. Using the diagram of the Sailboat block as a guide, draw the outline of the block onto the ruled-up square. Roughly colour in the boat, sail and background areas—this drawing will be the guide for cutting the correct number of pieces of each colour and for joining them together correctly.

On another piece of graph paper, draw a 3 inch (80 millimetre) square and a right-angle triangle with 3 inch (80 millimetre) sides. These will be the patterns, so they must be drawn very precisely with a sharp pencil. Draw another line exactly ¼ inch (6 millimetres) outside each side of the square and triangle. Do not cut out the shapes yet. Glue the graph paper to a sheet of lightweight card. When the glue is completely dry, cut out the shapes along the outer lines so that the ¼ inch (6 millimetre) seam allowance is included. The most accurate method is to use a craft knife and ruler.

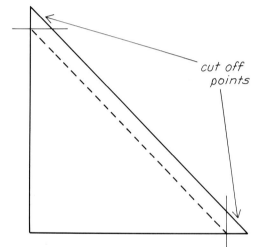

cut off
points

From the block diagram, decide how many squares and triangles of each colour will be needed. Place the cardboard templates on the wrong side of the fabric and draw around them with pencil. Make sure that one straight edge of the template is lined up with the grain of the fabric. Cut out the required number of pieces of each fabric.

Using the block diagram as a guide, lay the pieces out in their correct position. Pick up a pair of triangles and place right sides together. Sew the triangles together along the long side—note that this edge is on the bias of the fabric and will stretch very readily, so it should be handled gently. Join all the pairs of triangles and cut off the points as shown in the diagram. Press the seams to one side and replace the triangles, which have now been joined into squares, in their correct position.

Join the squares into four rows of four. Press the seams to one side. Alternate the direction in which the seams of the rows are pressed, which will make it easier to join the rows with the seams matching.

Join the rows into pairs, then join the pairs to complete the block. When joining the rows, pin carefully at each place where the seams meet. Press the seams to one side. Press the whole block from the right side.

Cut two border strips, each 2 × 12½ inches (50 × 332 millimetres). Sew to the top and bottom edges of the block. Cut another two border strips, each 2 × 16½ inches (50 × 445 millimetres). Sew to the sides of the blocks. Press the seams towards the borders.

Lay the needlepunch batting on top of the lining fabric then lay the completed block on the batting, right side up. Pin the three layers together and baste around the edges.

Hem one long edge of each of the pieces of backing fabric. Sew velcro along each hemmed edge and overlap the edges so that the velcro fastens. Place the completed cushion back and the three layers of the cushion front right sides together. Stitch around all four sides. Open the velcro

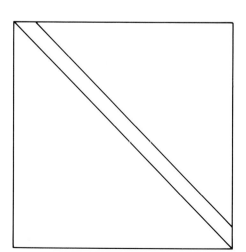

*Press triangles open,
seams to one side*

Four patch blocks

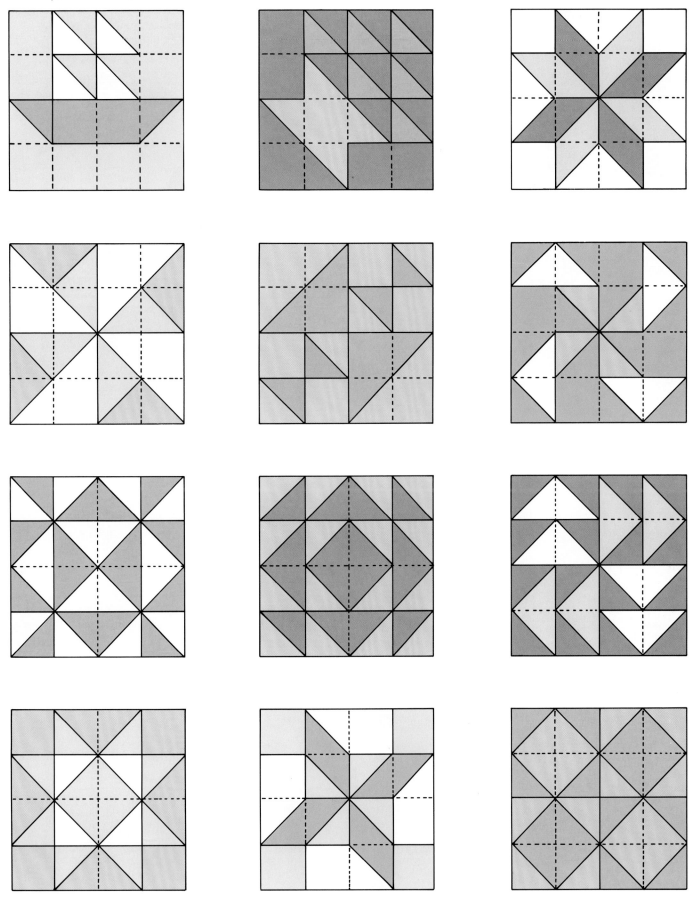

41

fastening and turn the cushion to the right side. Press gently. The cushion illustrated has not been quilted as this would be too difficult for a young sewer, but the layer of needlepunch batting gives the cushion a firm and professional finish. If made by a more experienced sewer, the cushion front could be MACHINE QUILTED before assembling the cushion.

Sew the two pieces of cushion insert fabric together, right sides facing, leaving an opening for turning. Turn and fill with polyester or wool and slipstitch the opening closed. Insert into the cushion.

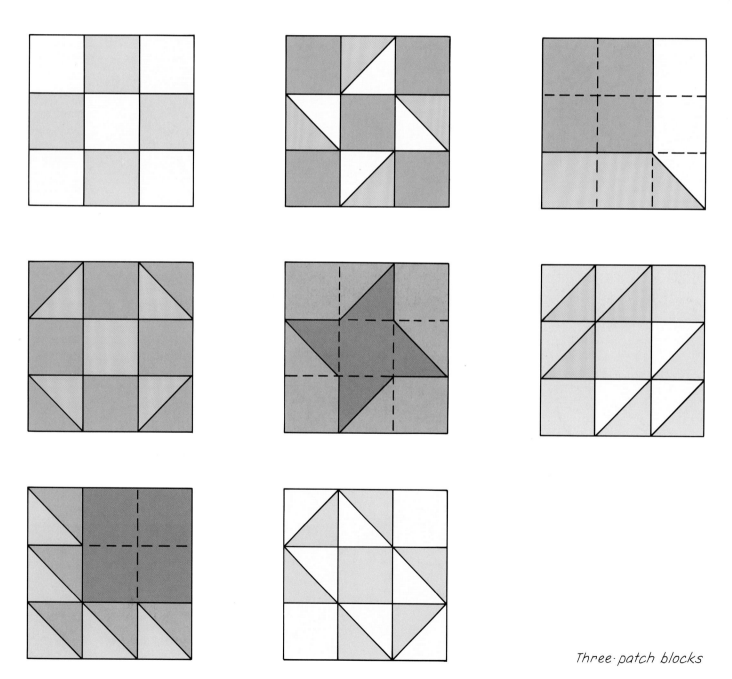

Three-patch blocks

Diagram 1

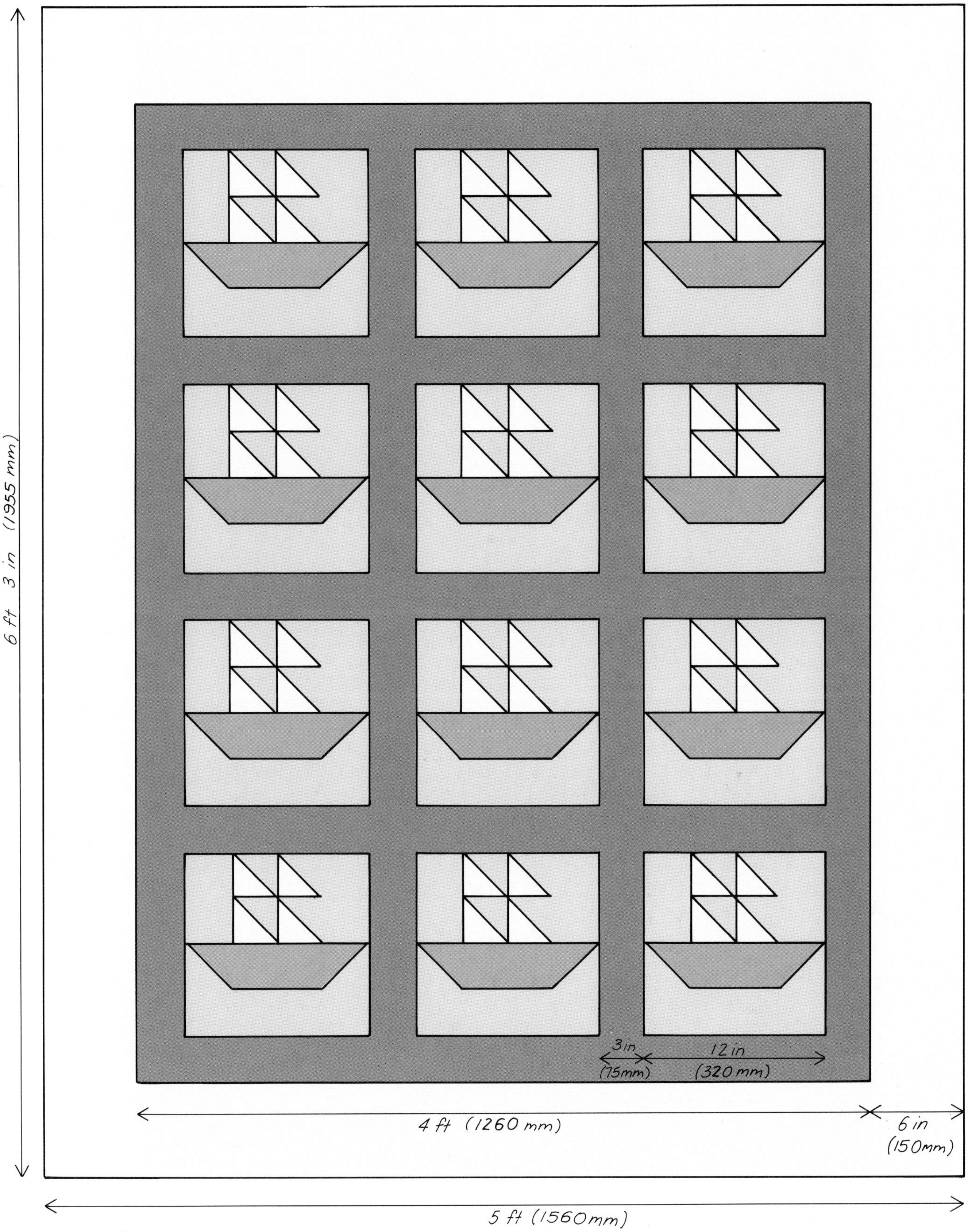

6 ft 3 in (1955 mm)

3 in
(75mm)

12 in
(320 mm)

4 ft (1260 mm)

6 in
(150mm)

5 ft (1560mm)

Add ¼ in seam allowance to all seams

PART TWO

ADVANCED PROJECTS

Kamon Quilts

The origin of the *kamon*, or family crest, goes back a long way in the history of Japan. They first appeared as patterns on the costumes and paraphernalia of the court aristocracy during the Nara period, AD 710-794, but by the twelfth century AD they had been taken up by the warrior class and used on the various trappings of war. As well, tradesmen used crests to decorate everything from toys and games, to cosmetics and cakes.

It is estimated that there are between 4000 and 5000 design variations and approximately 250 different subjects depicted in these crests. What a tremendous scope this offers to the quilter! Most libraries have an Asian section where reference books may be borrowed and the illustrations copied. Many of the designs are very simple and can be quite easily drawn up to the size of block required. The illustrations give some idea of the great variety of crests there are to inspire the quilter.

The blocks in the quilt shown are 12 inches (305 millimetres) square, the sashes are 2 inches (50 millimetres) wide and the borders measure 10 inches (255 millimetres). The finished quilt is 5 feet 4 inches × 7 feet 10 inches (1.62 × 2.40 metres), which is single bed size.

Patterns are given for five family crests (*mons* or *monsho*) depicted in the quilt illustrated. The first is scissors (*nasami*). Japanese scissors, unlike those of the western world, are formed from a single piece of metal and are operated by pinching the blades together. They first appeared as a design motif in the seventeenth century.

The second motif is a headdress. The many designs of hats led to them being used very often for family crests. They can be categorized as sedge hats (*kasa*), umbrella hats (*jingugasa* and *kasa hoko*), military hats (*ashigarugasa*, *jingasa*, and *amigasa*), cowls (*zuhin*), formal and semi-formal headdresses (*eboshi*) and battle helmets (*kabuto*).

The sedge hat (*kasa*) was worn by the nobles, so it was not surprising that the upper classes adopted and developed it as a design. The women and children of the nobility usually wore the *kasa* as a protection against rain, sun and snow.

The elaborate umbrella hats were reserved for wear on festive and religious occasions. They offered very effective concealment of the wearer's face.

Military hats were made of metal or thickly woven rush and were worn by low-ranking soldiers.

The cowl was originally worn under court headdress, but lovers found it very useful to hide their identity when going to a secret tryst. Not surprisingly, when the cowl was used as a design it came to be associated with the world of the pleasure quarters.

Formal and semi-formal headdresses developed gradually over a period of several centuries from the court headdress, which was associated with the system of "cap ranks". Court headdress was made of black silk and was worn in a certain way as befitted the wearer's rank. Gradually,

however, it began to be made of lacquered paper and became popular with the common people.

Although the very complex and ornate battle helmet had been worn for centuries, it was not until the late feudal period that it appeared as a crest. This is surprising, because the helmet was designed to protect not only the warrior's head, but his soul as well, as was evidenced by the religious emblems used on the helmets. Many helmets also carried horrific looking demons on them, designed to unnerve the opponents. These distinctive helmets meant that a warrior was easily identifiable in the heat of battle.

A third motif in the quilt is an umbrella (*kasa*). Umbrellas were made of oiled paper and split bamboo and were used against both the sun and the rain. The umbrella was originally a status symbol and only very gradually came to be used by the common people.

The fourth motif is a Shinto gateway (*torii*). The early mythology of Japan tells us that when the sun goddess went into a cave, thereby darkening the world, a cock sat outside crowing for her to come out again. Some scholars say that the Shinto gateway represents the perch on which the cock sat, and that the straw rope sometimes strung across the gateway was there to keep the goddess from re-entering the cave once she had been coaxed out.

The fifth motif is mist (*kasumi*). The stylized version of mist is seen often in Japanese scroll paintings and was a very popular decorative motif. It was adopted as a crest by some actors' families.

Further information can be found in a book by John W. Dower, *The elements of Japanese design: a handbook of family crests, heraldry and symbolism* (Walker/Weatherhill, 1971).

A selection of *kamon* are illustrated here, most of which have been chosen because they are suitable for applique, but some more elaborate designs are included to show the range encompassed by these beautiful crests. Patterns for some of the blocks used in the illustrated quilt are given, but designs of your choice can easily be drawn up to the required size from the pictures included here.

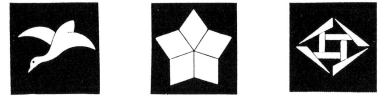

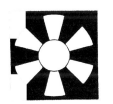

Half Scissors Block

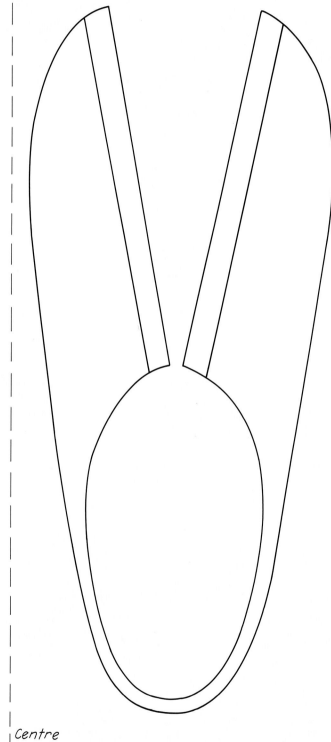

Centre

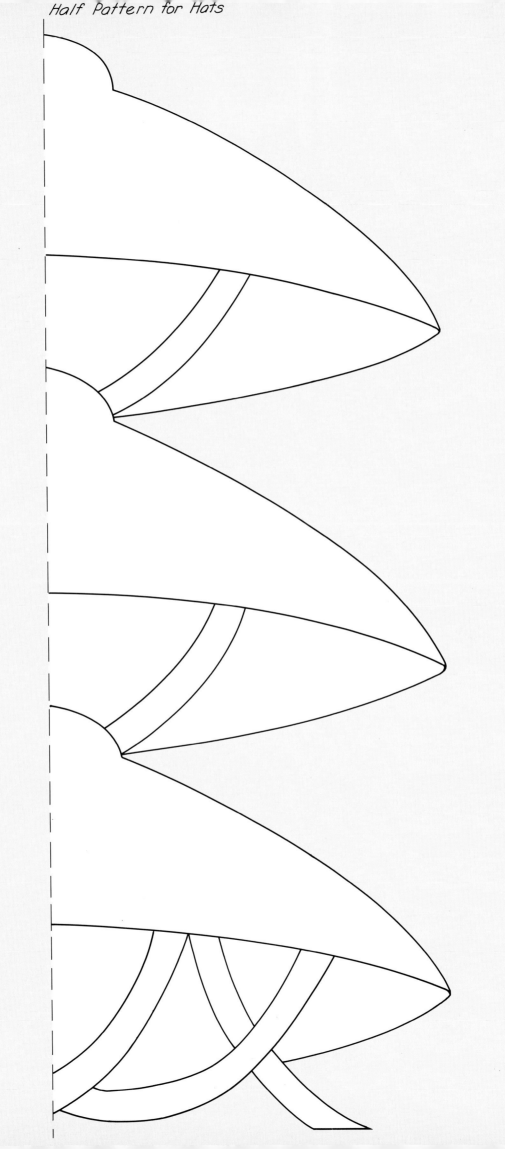

49

Umbrella Block

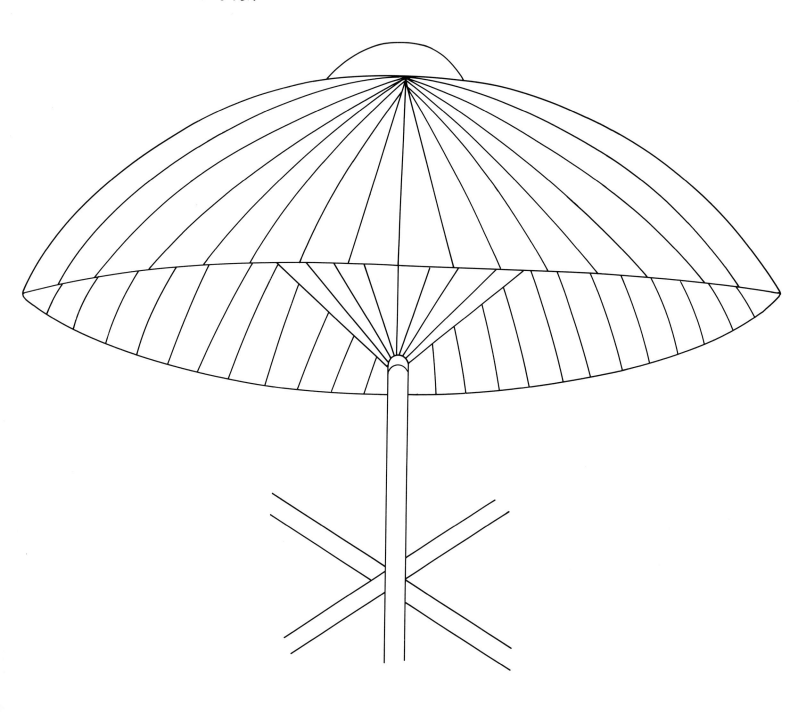

Half Pattern for Shrine Gate

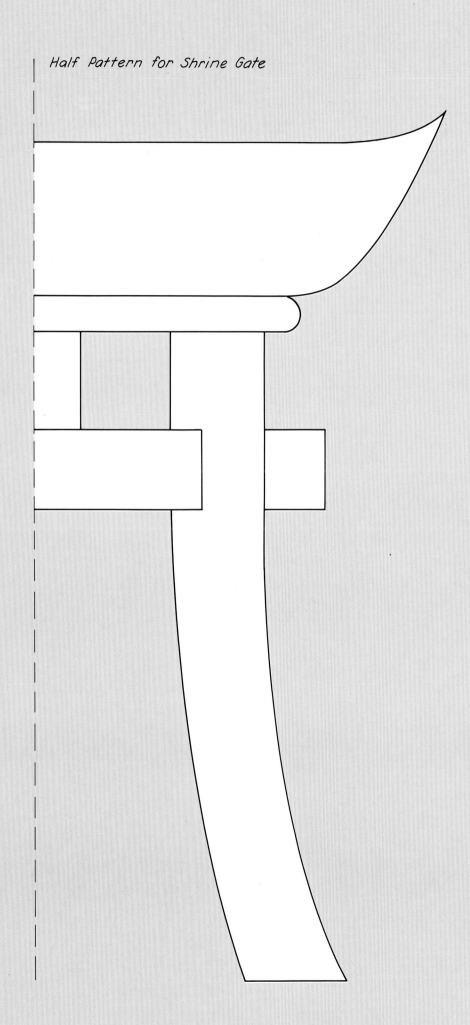

Half Pattern for Shrine Gate

51

Crescent Moon and Mist Block

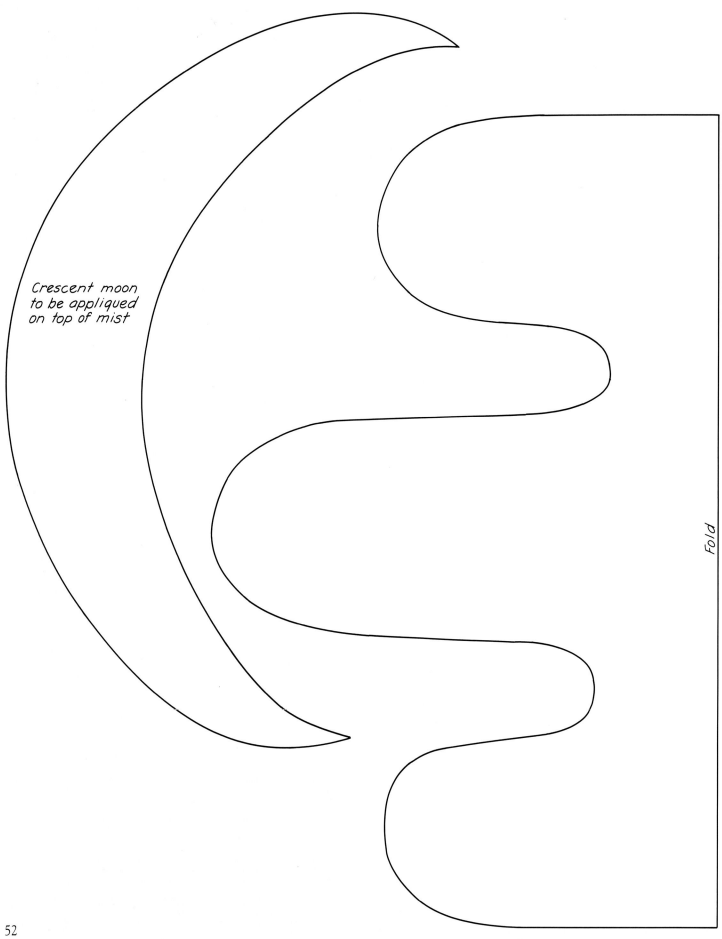

Crescent moon
to be appliqued
on top of mist

Fold

Sashiko Quilting

Sashiko quilting had a very practical origin. It was used to strengthen the homespun fabrics from which clothing was made. The need for warm clothing during Japan's long harsh winters inspired the idea of the lined kimono. Initially, the linings were of wild fibres and bracken, held together by the sashiko quilting, but they later progressed to layers of cotton material, again held together by the sashiko stitch.

A simple running stitch is used. At first just straight lines crossing or meeting at right-angles were used, but today there are many patterns, inspired by nature: pampas grass, hemp leaf and the Seven Buddhist Treasures (the seven treasures of Shippo Tsunagi are gold, silver, pearl, agate, crystal, coral and lapis lazuli), to name just a few. An example of sashiko quilting can be seen in the bottom left block of the photographed quilt.

Pampas Grass

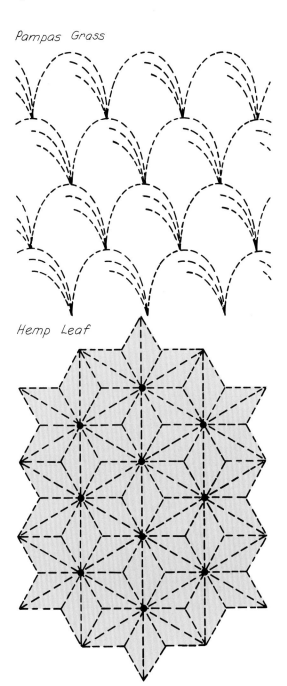

Hemp Leaf

Seven Buddhist Treasures design

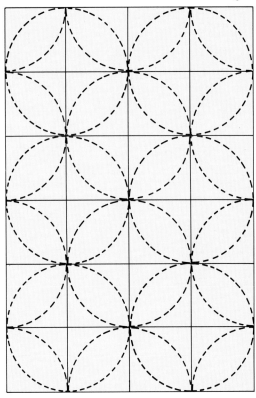

← 3/4 in (20 mm) →

Use a tracing wheel to mark a 3/4 in (20mm) grid on the piece to be quilted.
Use the grid as guidelines to draw circles with tailor's chalk or pencil and a 1½ in (38 mm) diameter template.
Use two or three strands of embroidery thread for quilting.

54

This wall quilt creates an interesting illusion of curving, wave-like motion even though all the pieces have straight edges. Colour balance is very important—three shades are required—light, medium and dark, and there must be good contrast between them. If the medium is too close in tone to the light or dark, the effect of the pattern will be lost.

Finished size: 42 inches (1.06 metres) square

MATERIALS

Dark fabric: 60 inches (1.5 metres) of 45 inch (115 centimetre) fabric
Medium fabric: 18 inches (50 centimetres) of 45 inch (115 centimetre) fabric
Light fabric: 2 yards (2 metres), which includes 45 inches (1.5 metres) for backing, of 45 inch (115 centimetre) fabric
Batting: 45 inches (1.15 metres) square

METHOD

MAKE TEMPLATES

Cut from dark fabric:
   64 pieces in shape F
   24 pieces in shape G
   Four border strips 2¾ × 45 inches (70 millimetres × 1.15 metres)
   16 feet (4.6 metres) of 2¼ inch (55 millimetre) bias strip for binding
Cut from medium fabric:
   9 pieces in shape A
   36 pieces in shape C
   16 pieces in shape D
Cut from light fabric:
   36 pieces in shape B
   64 pieces in shape E
   48 pieces in shape H
   48 pieces in shape Hr
   Four border strips 1½ × 40 inches (40 millimetres × 1.02 metres)

MACHINE PIECE one B to each side of every A. Press. Sew one C to each side of the AB squares, to make nine block 1 units.

Sew one E to each side of every D. Press. Sew one F to each side of the ED squares to make sixteen block 2 units.

Sew one H or Hr to each side of every G to make twenty-four block 3 units. Press.

Join four block 2 and three block 3 alternately to make a row, beginning with a block 2. Make three more rows the same as this.

Block 1

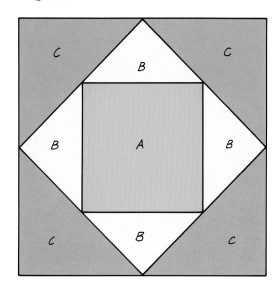

Join four block 3 and three block 1 alternately to make a row, beginning with a block 3. Make two more rows the same as this.

Join the rows alternately to complete the quilt top. Make sure that all seams meet exactly, unpick and adjust where necessary.

Sew one light border strip to each side, matching the centres. Note that extra length has been allowed on each border strip as insurance. MITRE THE BORDERS and trim excess fabric. Press. Sew and mitre the dark borders in the same manner. Press the top and trim the threads.

LAYER THE QUILT.

BIND THE EDGES.

HAND QUILT. Either outline quilt each patch or outline the shapes formed by the dark patches. You may prefer to quilt in an overall pattern of waving lines to emphasize the movement of the design, ignoring the outlines of the patches.

SIGN THE QUILT.

Block 2

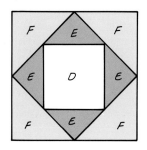

Block 3

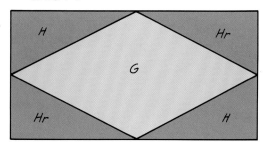

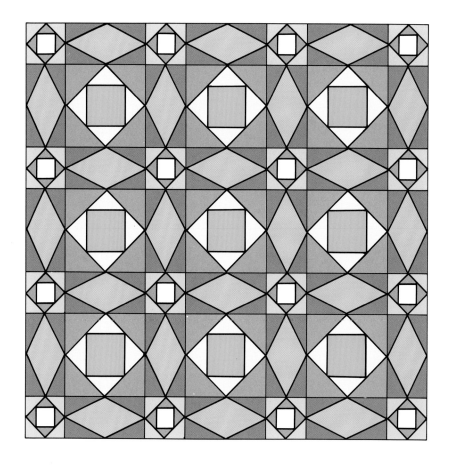

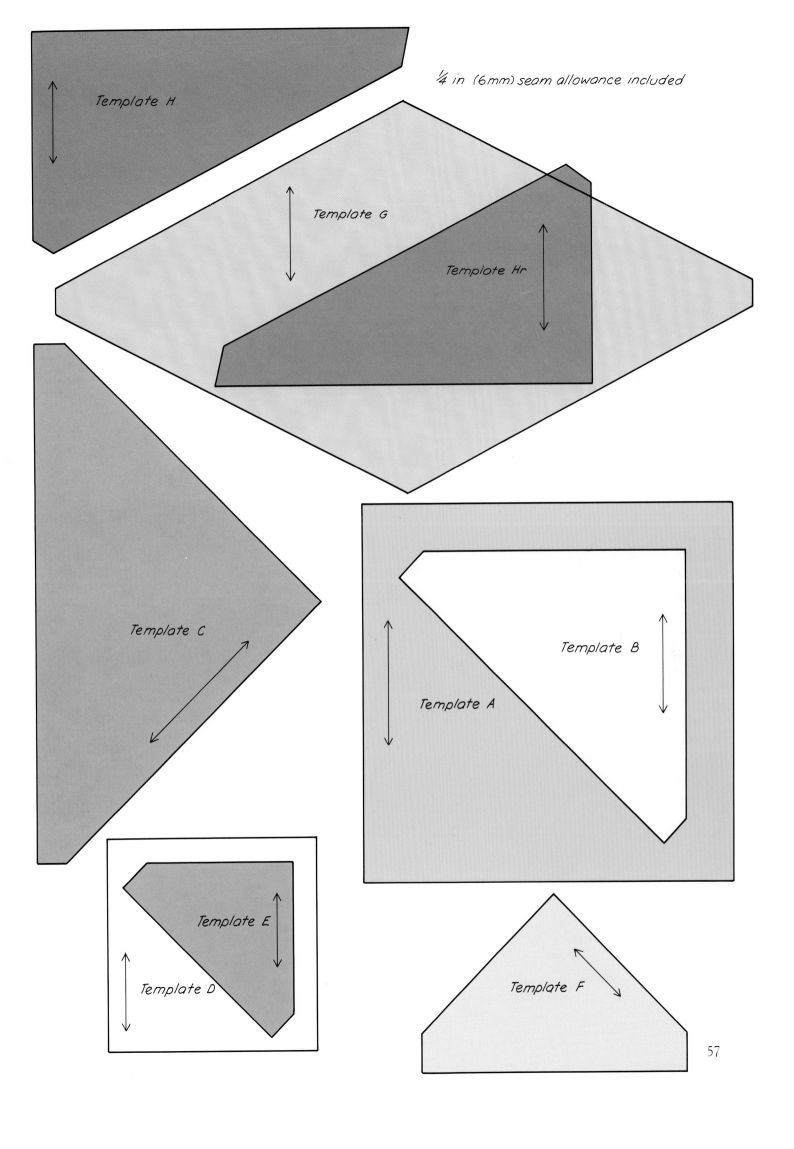

Template H

¼ in (6mm) seam allowance included

Template G

Template Hr

Template C

Template A

Template B

Template E

Template D

Template F

57

Hawaiian quilting is a unique style quite distinct from traditional American patchwork. Designs are cut from a large piece of fabric, usually folded into eighths, in the same way that snowflake patterns are cut from paper. The design is opened out and appliqued to a background fabric. It is then quilted with a contour or "echo" style of quilting, which radiates out from the appliqued design.

Authentic Hawaiian designs can be obtained by mail order from EA (Elizabeth Akana) of Hawaii, 150 Hamakua Drive, Suite 360, Kailua, Hawaii 96734. A catalogue* is available, which gives further information about Hawaiian quilting, pictures of the patterns available and a list of books and accessories. Two of the cushions and the cot quilt or wall hanging illustrated were made using patterns from EA of Hawaii.

Peigi has designed a pattern featuring a New Zealand native flower, the kowhai (*Sophora tetraptera*), so that you can try out the technique. If you would like to make your own design, look at the picture of the kowhai bloom and note how it has been modified to arrive at a design that is simple yet recognizable.

*The catalogue costs US$1.50.

Kowhai Cushion

Finished size: 18 × 18 inches (460 × 460 millimetres)

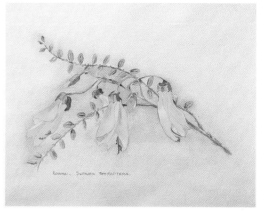

MATERIALS

Yellow/gold cotton fabric, 18 inches (460 millimetres) square
White cotton fabric for cushion front, 20 inches (505 millimetres) square
White cotton fabric for cushion back, two pieces each 19 × 12 inches (480 × 305 millimetres)
For cushion front: batting and lining, each 20 inches (505 millimetres) square
Piping cord covered with yellow fabric: 75 inches (1.95 metres)
Velcro: 18 inches (460 millimetres)
For cushion insert: two pieces of fabric, 20 inches (505 millimetres) square
For cushion filling: polyester or wool

METHOD

Pre-wash fabrics and press.

Lay the yellow fabric right side up and fold in half. Press. Fold in half again, quartering the fabric, and press. Fold diagonally so that the folded edges are together. Press. Baste along the folds.

Trace and cut out a paper pattern of the two pieces of the design. Place the patterns on the fabric so that the edges are aligned with the folds. Pin securely.

Cut out the patterns through all thicknesses of fabric, adding a 3/16 inch (8 millimetre) seam allowance. *Do not cut the folded edges.*

Fold and press the background fabric in the same manner. Open out flat, right side up. Unfold the applique fabric, being very careful not to stretch it. Lay the applique, right side up, on the background fabric. Match the bias and straight grain foldlines in the two fabrics. Pin thoroughly and baste the applique to the background. Leave the outer ¼ inch (6 millimetres) free so that the applique can be done without removing the basting.

HAND APPLIQUE the design in place, using a thread that is the closest possible match to the applique fabric.

Lay the cushion front over the lining and batting and baste all three layers together. Put the work into a quilting hoop and HAND QUILT as illustrated. Quilt around the applique, right next to the design but with the stitches in the background fabric, not the applique fabric. The next row of quilting should follow the shape of the design, about ½ inch (12 millimetres) further out.

When the quilting is finished, trim the front to 19 inches (480 millimetres) square. COMPLETE THE CUSHION.

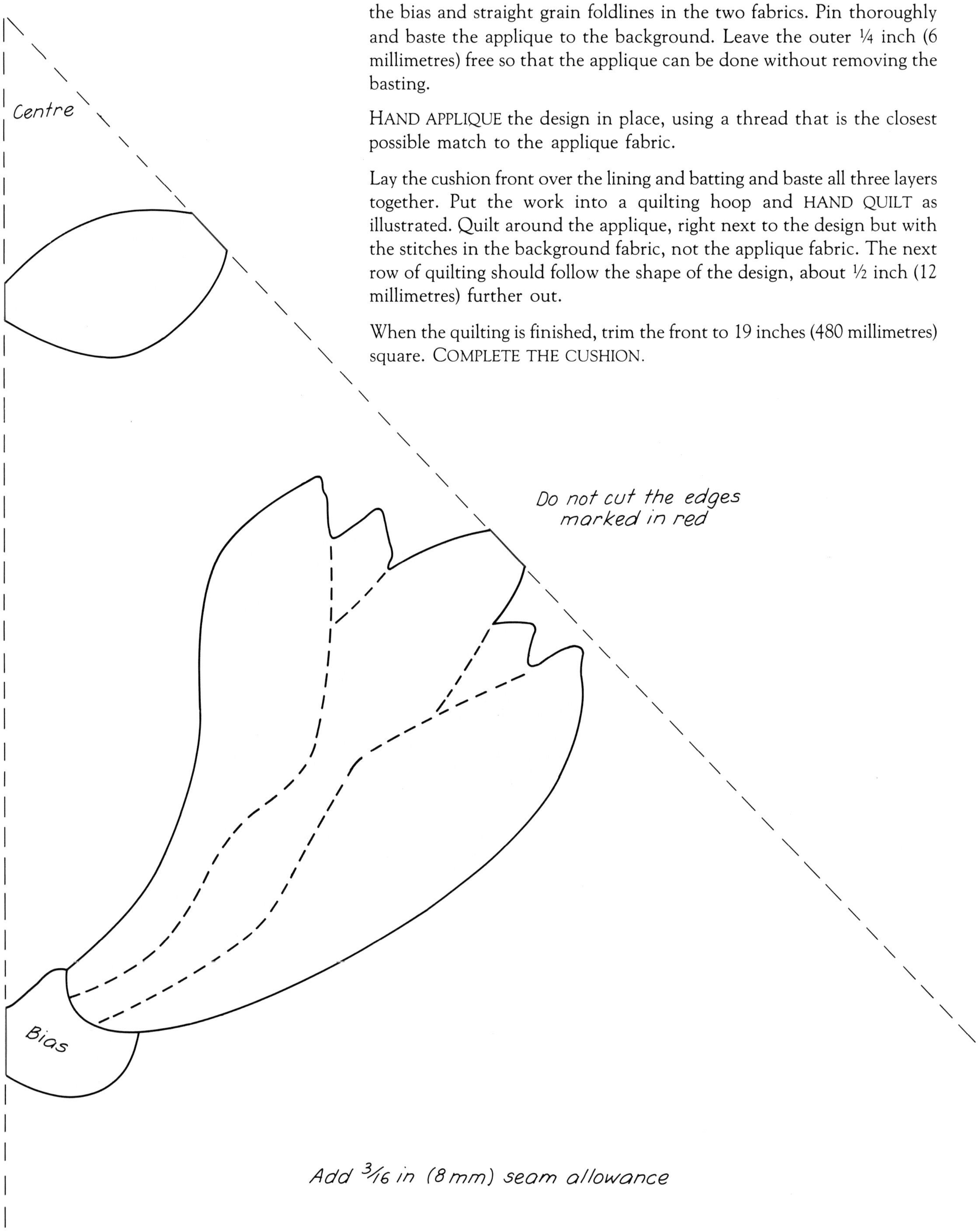

Centre

Do not cut the edges marked in red

Bias

Add ³⁄₁₆ in (8 mm) seam allowance

This cloth will lend a festive air to your table. Speciality patchwork shops and many fabric shops stock a range of Christmas print fabrics that can be combined with toning plain colours. The cloth is not difficult to sew and can be made in a size to suit your table simply by increasing the number of squares.

MATERIALS

Scraps of Christmas prints and a variety of red and green solid colours
3¼ yards (3 metres) of solid green fabric for outer border and backing
Four strips 1½ × 34 inches (38 × 864 millimetres) of light background print for inner border
Light-weight paper or organza type material to back squares

Diagram 1

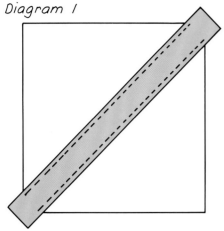

Diagram 2

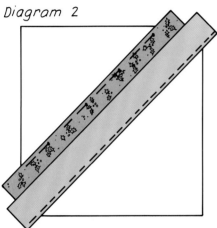

Diagram 3

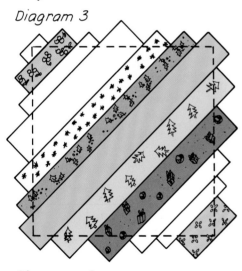

Diagram 4

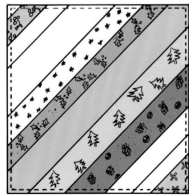

METHOD

Wash and press the fabric.

Cut the fabric into lengths of assorted widths between 1 and 3 inches (26 and 76 millimetres) on the straight grain of the fabric.

Cut twenty-five 6½ inch (166 millimetre) backing squares. If paper is going to be used, make sure it is light enough to tear away easily after sewing. A light organza was used in the cloth illustrated and was light enough to leave in, while adding almost no weight.

Sew a dark strip diagonally across one backing square. This is the only constant placement of colour whatever it may be (diagram 1). Place the second strip on top of the first strip, right sides together, and sew with ¼ inch (6 millimetre) seam. Turn over and finger press flat, and if necessary pin it down (diagram 2).

Continue in this way until the square is covered (diagram 3). Baste 1/8 inch (3 millimetre) from the outer edge. If used, tear away the paper backing and trim off excess fabric (diagram 4). Press. Continue until all twenty-five blocks have been sewn, remembering to start off with a dark strip, of any width, in the middle.

Join the blocks together in five horizontal rows of five blocks each. Press.

For inner borders sew a 1½ inch (38 millimetre) wide strip to each side, trim to fit, and press to outer edge. Sew the remaining strips to the top and bottom, trim and press.

For outer borders, cut four 8½ × 36 inch (260 × 914 millimetre) strips from the solid green fabric. Attach to cloth and press as for the narrow borders.

Three methods can be used to finish the cloth. For the first, cut the backing the same size as the top and machine baste around the edges. The illustrated tablecloth was finished by machine, using a scalloped edging.

Alternatively, place the top onto the backing, right sides together, and sew all round the edge, leaving a 6 inch (150 millimetre) gap for turning. Turn to the right side, slipstitch the gap, and press. Topstitch round the outer edges.

A third method would be to bind the edges. Cut 2 inch (50 millimetre) wide bias strips from the fabric. Measure the finished size of your cloth to determine how much binding to prepare. Press the bias strips in half lengthwise, wrong sides together and, with the raw edges of the binding even with the edges of the cloth, sew together with a ¼ inch (6 millimetre) seam. Turn the binding to the back and slipstitch in place.

Whichever method is used to finish the cloth, you should complete it by topstitching around both edges of the inner border. This should be sufficient to hold the top and backing together, but if it seems necessary, stitch in the ditch (on the right side stitch exactly along the seam line so that the stitches disappear in the seam) between every other row of blocks.

Quilting is an ideal communal activity. The many hours of work needed to produce a quilt can be reduced if the work is shared. There is also a special satisfaction in achieving something through group effort, and the time passes much more quickly with company.

There are many opportunities for making community quilts—such as centennial or jubilee celebrations of boroughs, cities or schools, the opening of a civic building, or refurbishing a historic home.

The authors were involved in making a community quilt as a gift to their local borough at the time of its centennial. That quilt is illustrated. The way the project was undertaken is described here as a source of ideas for any who would like to embark on something similar.

The Devonport Centennial Quilt

When centennial celebrations were being planned we approached the council with the suggestion of making a commemorative quilt. The council members were enthusiastic and agreed to assist with funding. They also provided the names of local people who owned textile companies who might give fabric. They responded generously, and so did a local quilt shop. As a result the quilt was produced using quality fabrics within the budget of $200.

The next step was to find helpers. Devonport is a small community with only a few committed quilters, but a number of volunteers were obtained through word-of-mouth. An article in a local newspaper attracted more helpers. The decision to divide the work into applique, embroidery and quilting meant that people who were skilled in only one aspect could still contribute. Other non-quilting skills were also useful, for instance, a local sign-writer drew up all the names of those involved in the quilt in an attractive script, which was embroidered in the borders. The greatest asset was a graphic artist who offered to help. She brought to the project skills that quilters do not necessarily have and was able to produce striking designs from ideas or sketches, which we could then translate into fabric.

Once funding and a team of workers were organized, attention was turned to the designs. Many people were asked what they considered were features of special importance to their community and a list was produced sufficient for three quilts. The list was reduced by eliminating ideas that could not easily be conveyed in fabric and by combining others. Books about the history of the area were consulted for information, drawings and photographs. Most of the designs were produced by the artist, except the centre panel, which was an enlargement of the council seal designed by one of the original councillors, and the examples of local architecture, which were drawn up using photograph negatives and an enlarger.

As the designs for the block were ready, they were given out first to those who were to do the applique. The fabric choice was made by

consultation between the volunteer and the co-ordinator, so that there was continuity and balance. Those doing applique took away the design and fabric and worked individually or in small groups. Some designs were more difficult than others, and those who were not confident about their ability were given the more straightforward designs or worked in a group. Nonetheless, the women who had very little confidence in their skill produced first class work.

After the applique was done, the designs were returned and handed to an embroiderer, unless the original worker wanted to do the complete block. While the blocks were being sewn, others were embroidering names on the borders. It was thought that those involved should be acknowledged, including those who had assisted with funding and other

64

non-sewing tasks. When the blocks were completed, the quilt top was assembled. This was the only stage at which the machine was used – the applique and quilting were entirely hand sewn.

The quilting was done in a large floor frame to minimize the handling of the quilt and to enable several quilters to work together. It should not be obvious that several quilters have worked on a quilt together because of noticeably different stitch lengths, so the less experienced quilters stitched around the blocks and "in the ditch". The completion date was rapidly approaching, so some very long days were spent bent over the frame, but it was very exciting to see the quilt nearly finished.

The final stitches were sewn only an hour before the unveiling ceremony. All the work seemed worthwhile to those who had taken part in a project that demonstrated that people can work together harmoniously and produce something better than any of them could have done alone. The quilt had taken exactly five months from the conception of the idea to completion. It had been very intensive work but it is often easier to maintain enthusiasm for a fast-moving project, than to work at a sensible pace for a lengthy period.

PRACTICAL ADVICE

Spend a lot of time planning and talking before even touching fabric. Establish exactly where funds and materials will come from, so that the project will not founder because either runs out. Determine who will provide the labour and how decisions will be made. Do not begin until you are confident that you have the materials and volunteers needed to complete the project.

Ask volunteers to keep in touch with the co-ordinator so that she knows that progress is being made. It is worrying when someone disappears with pattern and fabric and is not heard from. She is no doubt working steadily, but the co-ordinator needs to know this. If, for any reason, a volunteer cannot finish her part, she should ask for help or return the work for someone else to take over as soon as possible. Be understanding about the fact that unforeseen circumstances may prevent someone from doing as much as they had hoped to do.

Use only good quality fabric with the best possible fade resistance. Sometimes soft furnishing fabrics are more suited to prolonged exposure to light and dust than the usual fabrics used for patchwork.

In choosing the location for the finished quilt, select a situation that is not exposed to direct sunlight. Some sort of barrier to discourage the public from handling the quilt is also essential because the oils on even the cleanest hands will eventually discolour and damage the fabric.

The method of hanging the quilt also needs to be considered. The Devonport quilt was hung as follows and it has been very successful. Strips of velcro 1 inch (25 millimetres) shorter than each side were sewn to bands of calico. The calico was ½ inch (12 millimetres) wider than the velcro, so that the bands could be stitched to the back of the quilt. They were stitched by hand through the calico only, and not through the velcro, which is difficult to sew through by hand. One velcro band was attached to each of the four sides. The matching pieces of velcro were stapled to timber battens. One batten was screwed to the wall at the top and the quilt attached to it. The bottom batten was positioned so that the quilt

would be held under very slight tension so that it was perfectly smooth, but not taut. The side battens were then positioned so that the quilt was held out to its full width. Neither the battens nor the velcro should be visible when the quilt is hanging. This method of hanging supports the quilt well and does not allow all the stress to be taken by the top edge. Another advantage is that the quilt could be rapidly removed from the wall in the event of fire by simply ripping it down, without a ladder or tools being needed.

PICTORIAL APPLIQUE

We soon found that applique of existing scenes and objects that you want to be recognizable to viewers demands a slightly different approach from decorative applique. Embroidery is necessary to convey small details, such as the name of a boat or the wording of a sign. Lurex thread and net were used for the water cascading from a fountain; lurex thread also gave sparkle to a comet and net was used for the smoke from a ship's funnel. Ribbon, braid and other trims provide interesting textures and can be used for balustrading and fretwork on buildings. Fabric designs can often be found that are ideal for roofing iron, picket fences, bricks and paving. The photographs of individual blocks show the use of embroidery, trims and fabric design to achieve realistic effects.

Be very careful about any lettering used — it will detract from the appearance of the quilt if it is not absolutely precise. The method we used, after much experimentation, was as follows. A sign-writer's alphabet sheet was obtained in a suitable size and style. The letters were traced onto iron-on interfacing, which was applied to the wrong side of the fabric. The interfacing was not only a method of transferring the letters, but it also reinforced the fabric and reduced fraying of the edges. The letters were carefully cut out and positioned on the background fabric and basted in place. The edges were overcast with a narrow, close zigzag stitch. The fabric used for the letters should be firm and closely woven so that it holds its shape and does not fray excessively. A heavy embroidery thread was then threaded from the wrong side of the fabric and couched around the edge of each letter and secured with tiny stitches in a fine matching thread. The heavy thread was returned to the wrong side at the end of each letter and the ends secured by whipstitching to the underside of the fabric with the fine thread. The couching thus covers the overcasting stitches. The script for the names was drawn onto the fabric using a light box and embroidered by couching with heavy thread over the marked outline.

A wholecloth quilt is made from a piece of plain fabric that is quilted extensively. The entire design is quilted – there is no piecing or applique. This technique is well suited to those who enjoy the quilting more than any other stage of making a quilt and it shows off elaborate motifs to advantage. The quilting is a joy to do because there are no seams or multiple layers of fabric to quilt through. Fabrics with a sheen, such as silk, satin or chintz, are an excellent choice for wholecloth work because they show the quilting very well, but cotton or lawn, such as that used for the illustrated quilt, are equally suitable.

Finished size: 32 × 24 inches (810 × 610 millimetres)

MATERIALS

For top: 32 inches (80 centimetres) of cotton, silk, satin or chintz 45 inches (115 centimetres) wide
For backing: 32 inches (80 centimetres) fabric, 45 inches (115 centimetres) wide
Batting: 28 inches (70 centimetres) of wool or tetron
For binding: 30 inches (75 centimetres) of matching or contrasting fabric

METHOD

On a large sheet of paper, draw a rectangle 32 × 24 inches (810 × 610 millimetres). Draw another rectangle 3 inches (70 millimetres) inside the first. Mark the centre lines on the paper and trace the heart motif. Trace the other motifs, positioning them as shown in the photograph. Use a felt pen so that the outline is clear enough to trace onto the fabric. Do not mark the cross-hatching, as masking tape will be used for this.

Pre-wash the fabrics and press. Do not cut out any of the fabric—the full 32 inches (80 centimetres) are used and trimmed later. Lightly press centre lines in the top fabric. Place over the paper pattern and match crease lines to centre lines and pin the fabric to the paper. Use a fine, soft pencil and trace the motifs with a dotted line. The markings must obviously be clear enough to see when quilting, but should not be any darker than necessary.

LAYER THE QUILT.

Do not cut off the excess material. It is easier to position the quilt in a hoop or frame when quilting near the edges of the design if there is extra fabric.

HAND QUILT the motifs. A quilting hoop is best for this, but if you have a floor frame, you may wish to transfer the quilt to it when quilting the diagonal cross-hatching and straight-line borders.

Place a 45 degree set square in one corner of the quilt and run a strip of masking tape along its long edge. Quilt either side of the tape and mark the position of the remaining lines with masking tape. Check occasionally with the set square that the lines are still meeting the sides of the quilt at a 45 degree angle. The cross-hatching should cover the entire background, but should not continue across the motifs. The purpose of the cross-hatching is to flatten the background and emphasize the raised areas of the motifs. Quilt the border lines and use ¼ inch (6 millimetre) masking tape to mark a line ¼ inch (6 millimetres) inside the border lines.

When the quilting is complete, remove the basting threads and BIND THE QUILT.

SIGN THE QUILT. You may wish to embroider the name and birth date of the baby in the large centre heart.

Seminole patchwork is a form of strip-piecing in which long strips of fabric are sewn together to form multicoloured bands, which are then cut into segments, arranged to form geometric designs, and sewn again, producing a patterned band that can be incorporated into clothing or other items. Finished seminole work looks very intricate because it is made up of many tiny pieces of fabric, but it is not difficult because the method of construction does not require any of the small pieces to be handled individually.

Seminole Bands on Towels

Three different fabrics were used for the seminole strip on the illustrated towel, but the number of fabrics used is entirely a matter of choice. It is advisable to pre-wash the fabrics under the same conditions that the towel will be washed to check that they will be suitable.

All measurements include ¼ inch (6 millimetre) seam allowance and 45 inch (115 centimetre) wide fabric was used. The design will make a 2¼ × 36 inch (57 × 915 millimetre) band.

Accurate cutting is essential. Fold the fabric in four widthways and mark the required number of strips with either a fine ballpoint, or a well sharpened soft pencil. Cut out carefully with scissors, or use a heavy plastic ruler and a rotary cutter, which will be much quicker.

Diagram 1

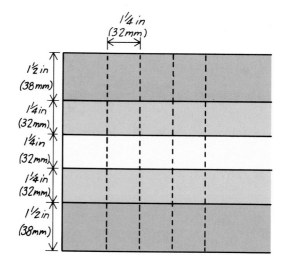

METHOD

Cut: Fabric A: one strip, 1½ × 45 inches (39 millimetres × 115 centimetres)

Fabric B: two strips, 1½ × 45 inches (39 millimetres × 115 centimetres)

Fabric C: two strips, 1½ × 45 inches (39 millimetres × 115 centimetres)

Sew the strips into a band and press all the seams in the same direction. Turn the band to the right side and press again, making sure that no tucks have been ironed in along the scam lines.

Mark a perpendicular line at the left side of the band and mark and cut the pieces as shown in diagram 1.

Sew the pieces together, carefully aligning the seams, as shown in diagram 2. The most efficient way to join the pieces is by CHAIN SEWING. First of all sew the pieces in pairs without cutting the thread. When all the pairs are joined, clip the threads and open the pairs up. Once again align the seams and sew two pairs together, again not cutting the thread. Continue doing this until the whole band is sewn (diagram 3).

Press all the seams in the same direction, again turning over and pressing from the right side to eliminate any creases.

Mark lines ¼ inch (6 millimetres) above and below the squares in the design and trim (diagram 4).

Edging strips are used to finish off the raw edges of the band, and also to simplify attaching the band to the towel. The edging strips on the towel illustrated were cut 7/8 inches (23 millimetres) wide, allowing for ¼ inch (6 millimetre) seams, but any width strips may be used. Cut the strip the same length as the band.

Align the edging strips to the cut edges of the band and sew in a ¼ inch (6 millimetre) seam, top and bottom (diagram 5).

Turn under ¼ inch (6 millimetre) seam and sew the band to the towel. This may be firmly hand sewn, or topstitched by machine.

Diagram 2

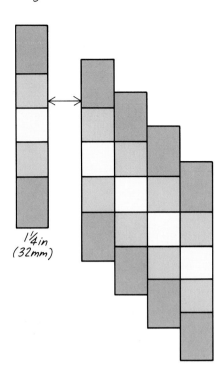

1¼in
(32mm)

Diagram 3

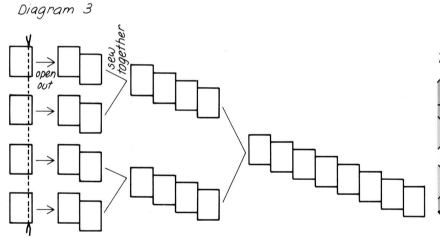

open out

sew together

Diagram 4

Trim ¼in (6mm) above and below squares

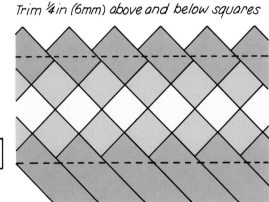

Diagram 5

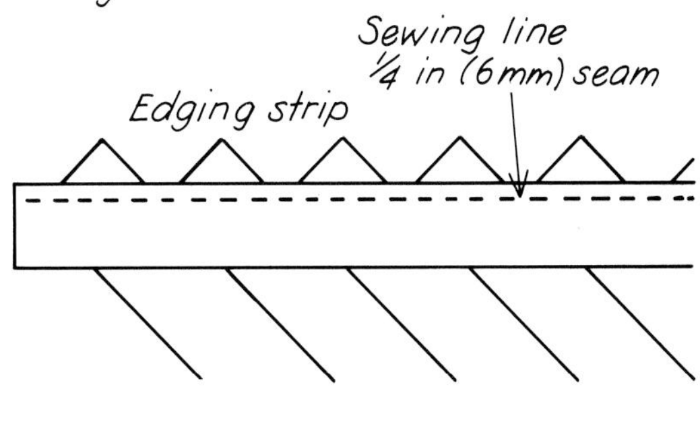

Sewing line
¼ in (6mm) seam

Edging strip

Seminole Bands on an Artist's Roll

This roll, designed to hold paintbrushes, can very easily be adapted for pencils, knitting needles or crochet hooks.

The same seminole design as for the towel was used, but the scale was doubled. This is easier to do than it seems (diagram 6).

HOW TO ALTER THE SCALE OF THE DESIGN

Subtract the ¼ inch (6 millimetre) seam allowance, which is a total of ½ inch (12 millimetres) from each strip width.

Halve, double or treble the original width measurement (do not make life difficult for yourself by using fractions), then add the seam allowance back on, ¼ inch (6 millimetres) on each side, a total of ½ inch (12 millimetres).

Follow the same procedure with the cut pieces as for the towel. Subtract the seam allowances from each side, multiply by the amount decided upon, then add the seam allowances back on.

MATERIALS

Canvas or other firm material: 16 × 12 inches (405 × 305 millimetres)
                               16 × 5 inches (405 × 125 millimetres)
                               15 × 5 inches (380 × 125 millimetres)
Seminole strip 17 × 5¼ inches (435 × 134 millimetres)
2 edging strips 17 × 4 inches (435 × 102 millimetres)
Bias binding: 55 inches (1.4 metres)

METHOD

Mark the 16 × 5 inch (405 × 125 millimetre) flap into divisions. Vary the widths of these to accommodate different size brushes. Be sure to leave a division wide enough for a craft knife. Neaten the inner edge of this piece.

Attach to the main piece on the long side by sewing along the marked lines. It is not necessary to sew the outer edge, as this will be caught in later by the seminole strip (diagram 7).

Neaten one long edge and the two short edges of the second flap and tack to the other long side of the main piece (diagram 7).

Make the seminole band in the same manner as the guest towel. Check the finished size, and if necessary, alter the width of the edging strips to ensure that the finished size is not less than the 16 × 12 inches (405 × 305 millimetres) measurement of the main canvas piece.

Place the right side of the seminole strip face down on the outside of the canvas piece and sew down the two long edges, being careful not to catch in the short side of the loose canvas flap. Turn out to the right side and press the seams flat. Topstitch the seams.

Bind the two open ends with bias binding. Sew the edges of the remaining bias binding together and attach to one end as ties.

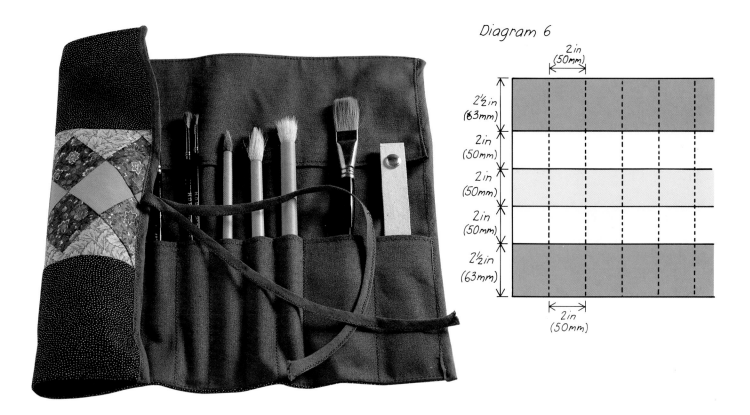

Diagram 6

2in
(50mm)

2½in
(63mm)

2in
(50mm)

2in
(50mm)

2in
(50mm)

2½in
(63mm)

2in
(50mm)

Diagram 7

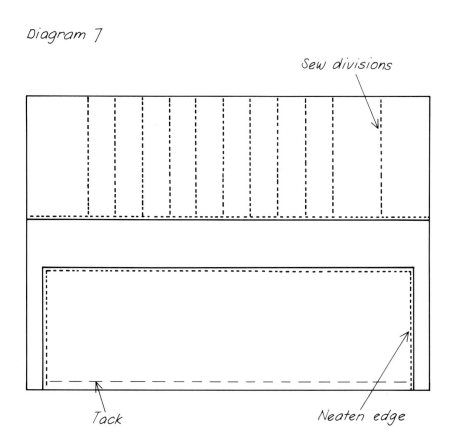

Sew divisions

Tack

Neaten edge

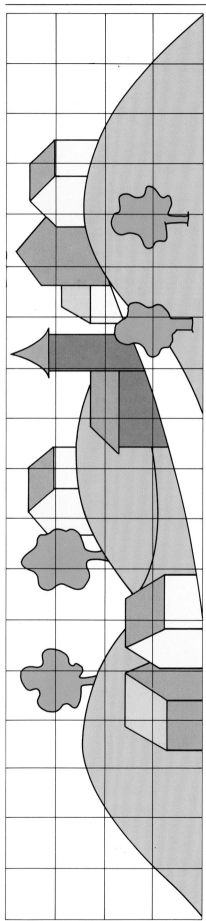

Each square = 2in (50mm)

This baby mat, which could also be used as a cot quilt, features an appliqued town scene. It is very versatile as it can be hand or machine appliqued and quilted. Make it in assorted print fabrics as shown or in bright plain colours.

Finished size: 43½ inches (1.1 metres) square

MATERIALS

2 5/8 yards (2.4 metres) blue cotton fabric, 45 inches (115 centimetres) wide
Small quantities of assorted cotton fabrics
½ yard (40 centimetres) brown ribbon for the tree trunks
Batting 1 1/3 yards (1.22 metres) square
Metric graph paper ruled with 5 centimetre squares
Carbon paper
Tracing paper

METHOD

To enlarge the pattern to full size, copy it square by square onto the graph paper.

Cut two pieces of blue cotton for the front and back, each 44½ inches (1.13 metres) square.

On one piece, mark a line 4½ inches (115 millimetres) in from the edge all round. Using the carbon paper, transfer the applique design on each of the four sides, lining up the lower edge of the design with the line marked on the fabric. Or transfer the design using a LIGHT BOX.

Trace the motifs onto the paper and cut out. Using these as patterns, cut out each shape in the coloured fabrics four times. If you are using a light box, trace the outline of the shape onto the right side of the fabric and cut out. The play mat illustrated was hand appliqued, so a small seam allowance was added when cutting out the fabrics. It is not necessary to add a seam allowance if the mat is to be machine appliqued.

MACHINE APPLIQUE or HAND APPLIQUE, beginning with the meadows and hills, then add houses and trees.

Pin the front and the back of the mat together, right sides facing. Pin the batting to these and machine stitch all around, leaving a gap for turning. Turn right side out and slipstitch the opening closed. Alternatively, baste the layers together, right sides out and BIND THE EDGES.

To finish, HAND QUILT around the base of the applique, the edge of the hills, houses and trees. The mat illustrated was hand quilted, but MACHINE QUILT if you prefer.

This design was inspired by Pauline Adams' winning entry in a quilt design contest held to celebrate the fifteenth anniversary of the *Quilter's Newsletter Magazine*. I have drafted a pattern for a wall hanging. The design is most attractive and not at all difficult to piece. It would make a lovely single bed quilt if based on a 6 inch (150 millimetre) block instead of the 4 inch (100 millimetre) block used for the wall hanging.

The illustrated quilt was made using silk for the flowers because of its sheen and beautiful, vibrant colours. The glazed finish of chintz or polished cotton would give a similar effect.

Finished size: 35 ✕ 51 inches (900 millimetres ✕ 1.3 metres)

MATERIALS

Silk or other fabric: 12 inches (30 centimetres) of 45 inch (115 centimetre) fabric in seven different colours
2 2/3 yards (2.5 metres) of 45 inch (115 centimetre) cotton fabric for background and backing
18 inches (450 millimetres) satin for ribbon
18 inches (450 millimetres) green cotton fabric for stems
1½ yards (1.4 metres) cotton fabric for borders and binding
1 yard (1 metre) batting

METHOD

Photocopy or trace the assembly chart and colour the flowers according to your choice of fabrics. The quilt will be assembled according to this chart and it is much easier to assemble correctly if the chart is coloured to correspond to your fabrics. The chart also gives you an idea of the finished effect of your choice of colours – rearrange the colours until you are happy with them.

MAKE TEMPLATES.

From the chart, count how many pieces of each shape must be cut from each fabric. The entire design can be pieced into 4 inch (100 millimetre) squares, which are then joined to form the quilt top. You may prefer to reduce the number of seams by combining areas that use the same fabric. For example instead of cutting three pieces of F for the left end of the bottom row, you could cut one piece measuring 4½ ✕ 12½ inches (115 ✕ 320 millimetres).

Cut out the required number of pieces. It is preferable to cut the four petals of the flowers so that the grain will run the same way through the block once they are joined, especially if the fabric has a different colour appearance when viewed according to the way in which the grain runs. If you use a cotton fabric for the flowers, all the petals can be cut according to the grain line marked on the template. But if there is colour variation

with the fabric you are using, cut one petal with the point directed upwards, rotate the template 90 degrees and cut the next petal. Rotate the template a further 90 degrees before cutting each of the remaining two petals. Lay the pieces out in their correct position, or label them so that they do not get mixed up after you have gone to the trouble of cutting them in this manner. The pieces need not be cut individually because three or four different colours can be layered and cut out together if their straight edges are aligned.

The dotted lines divide the chart into 4 inch (100 millimetre) blocks. Beginning with the top row, assemble the blocks according to the chart. Join the blocks to form rows. Press.

Join the rows to form six pairs. Join the pairs to form three 4-row sections then join these to complete the piecing. Joining the rows in this way is less bulky than adding each row to all the previous rows.

Be sure that all the seams meet exactly. Unpick where necessary and adjust.

Cut two border strips 1¾ × 38 inches (45 × 960 millimetres) and two 1¾ × 54 inches (45 millimetres × 1.37 metres). Extra length is included as insurance. ATTACH THE BORDERS, making mitred corners. Trim off any excess fabric.

Press the entire top carefully. Trim any threads so that they will not show through the completed quilt.

LAYER THE QUILT.

BIND THE QUILT using 2¼ inch (60 millimetre) bias strips cut from the border fabric.

HAND QUILT as shown in the quilting and colour chart. The ribbon can be outline quilted or the vine motif can be used. Quilt the background using the teacup design if desired.

SIGN THE QUILT.

TO MAKE A SINGLE BED QUILT

Construct in the same manner, using the templates for a 6 inch (150 millimetre) block. Increase the width of the borders to 6 inches (150 millimetres). The finished size will be 5 × 7 feet (1.52 × 2.15 metres).

Teacup quilting

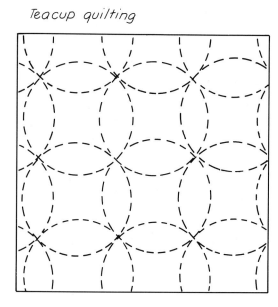

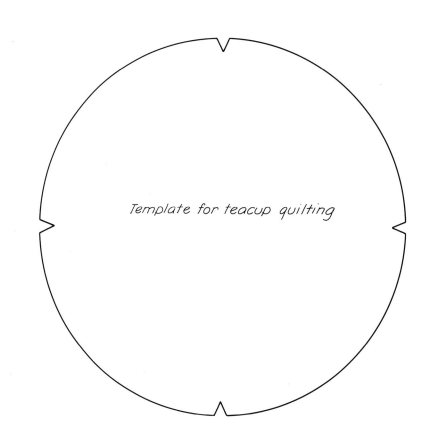

Template for teacup quilting

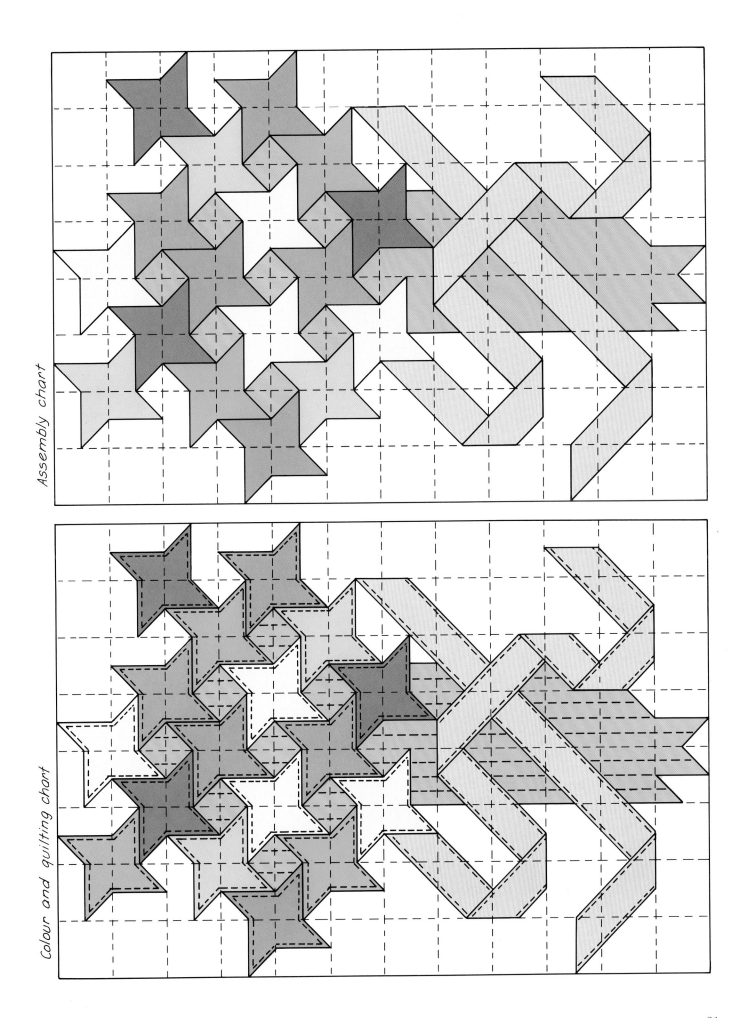

Assembly chart

Colour and quilting chart

81

Templates for Friendship Bouquet, for 4 in (100mm) block for wall quilt
¼ in (6mm) seam allowance included

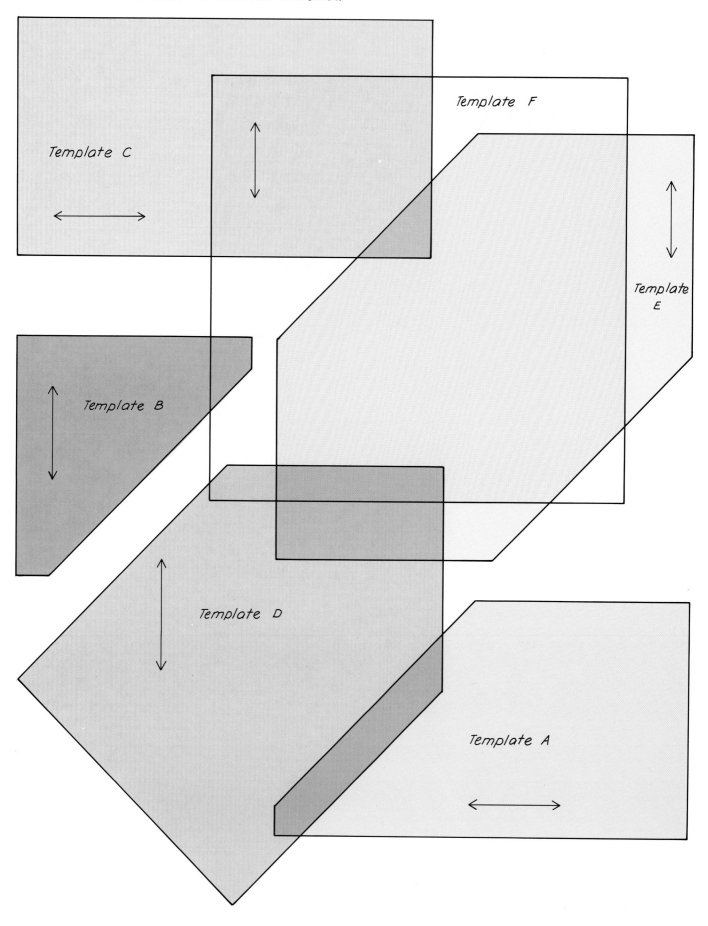

Template C

Template F

Template E

Template B

Template D

Template A

Templates for Friendship Bouquet, for 6 in (150 mm) block for bed quilt
¼ in (6 mm) seam allowance included

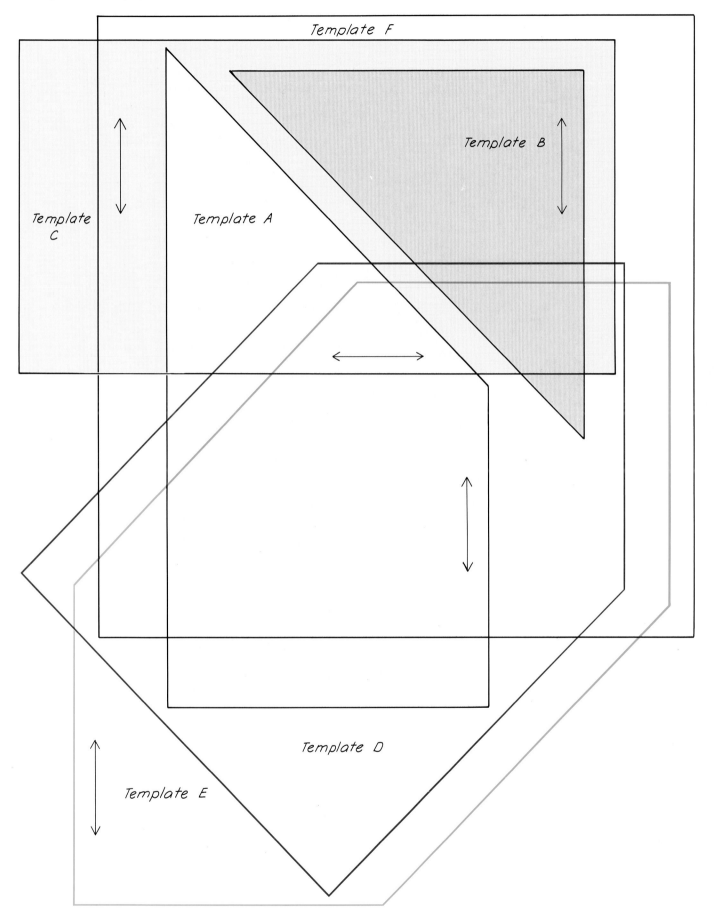

Template F

Template B

Template C

Template A

Template D

Template E

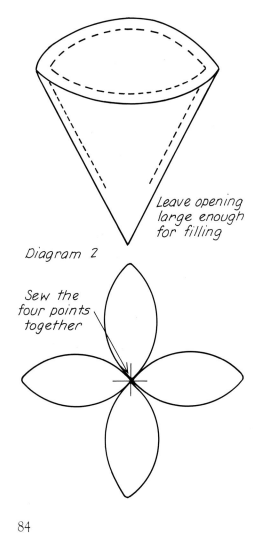

A soft ball with lots of places for tiny fingers to grasp.

MATERIALS

Scraps of brightly coloured cotton prints and solids
Polyester or wool for filling

METHOD

Cut twelve pieces of shape A and twenty-four pieces of shape B.

Sew two B pieces, right sides together, leaving an opening at the point large enough for filling.

With the right sides together sew one top to the two B pieces (diagram 1).

Continue until twelve triangles have been sewn.

Turn to the right side, stuff with filling, and stitch the opening closed.

Using a needle and strong thread, sew through all twelve points of the triangles until they are all strung together. Tie the ends of the thread firmly so that the points are pulled together in the centre.

Take four adjoining triangles and sew them together at their points (diagram 2).

Select one of these pieces and sew three new triangles to its remaining point to make another cluster of four.

Continue until all twelve pieces have been joined together.

Diagram 1

Leave opening
large enough
for filling

Diagram 2

Sew the
four points
together

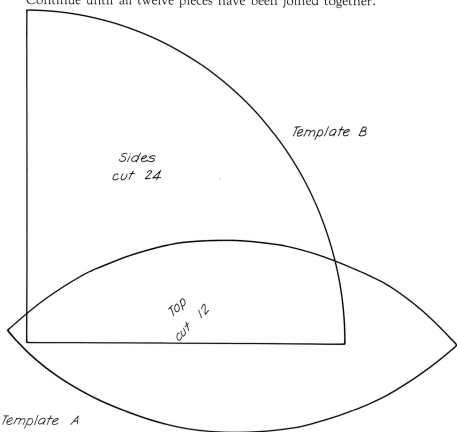

Template B

Sides
cut 24

TOP
cut 12

Template A

Leather is a wonderful material for patchwork, especially now that soft garment leather is available that can be cut and sewn as easily as fabric. Patchwork can make use of scraps that would otherwise be of no use. Unlike fabric, leather does not fray so seam allowances need not be turned under. Synthetic suede would also be very suitable if obtainable, and it also has the advantage of being washable.

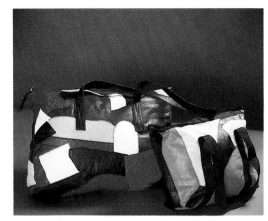

If you wish to sew leather, it is advisable to talk to your sewing machine dealer, who can advise about suitable needles, feet, thread and stitches. The bags illustrated were sewn on a Bernina 930 machine, using a leather needle and a walking foot.

The first step is to make up the leather patchwork, then make it into a bag using a commercial pattern. Most pattern companies offer suitable bag patterns, like the one used here. Alternatively, a simple pattern can be made from a rectangle equal in width to the desired width and twice the desired length. A zip is inserted between the top edges and the side seams sewn, as described in the diamond patchwork bag instructions.

Leather Crazywork

Soft garment leather must be used for this because the machine must be able to sew easily through two layers of leather plus the lining fabric to make the patchwork, and then sew through a double thickness when making up the bag.

Cut a piece of lining fabric larger than each piece required for your chosen bag pattern. Draw the outline of each pattern piece on the fabric. Beginning at the top edge of one piece of lining fabric, place a patch face up on the fabric. Place another piece overlapping the first by approximately ¼ inch (6 millimetres). Use short lengths of masking tape or glue stick to hold the patches in place. Sew along the overlapped edge with a zigzag stitch. The stitching should all be on the upper patch, with the needle extending just past the raw edge on its right hand swing. This way the edge is neatly secured. Trim any excess leather from beneath the upper patch. Continue to add patches, overlapping the previous patches and sewing along the upper edge. The lower edges will be secured when the next patch is added. Take care when adding a patch to do it with the work laid out on a flat surface, secure the patch with masking tape, and transfer the work to the sewing machine without disturbing the position, otherwise the crazywork could become puckered. When the outlined area on the lining fabric has been completely covered, lay the pattern piece on the reverse side and draw around it. Stitch all around, just inside the marked line, to secure the edges, then cut out. When all pattern pieces have been made and cut out, make up the bag according to the pattern instructions. Note that insertion of the zipper is much easier if an open-ended zipper is used, because it can be separated and each half of the zipper sewn to the bag individually, then joined. You may prefer to insert the zipper between two lengths of webbing, then sew the webbing to the bag so that the edge of the webbing overlaps the raw edge of the leather.

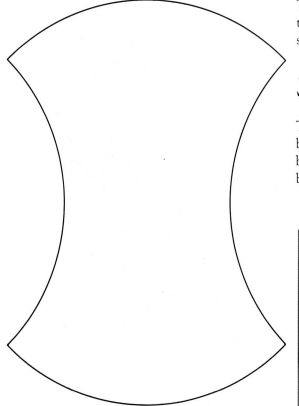

Spool Template
Based on 3 in (75 mm) square

This produces a neat appearance and the same webbing can be used for the handles. If you sew the zipper directly to the leather, position and secure it with glue stick before stitching.

Spools Bag

This bag was made from the same commercial pattern as the crazywork bag, but a different type of patchwork is used. The pieces of leather are butted edge to edge and sewn together. A heavier grade leather should be used for this bag.

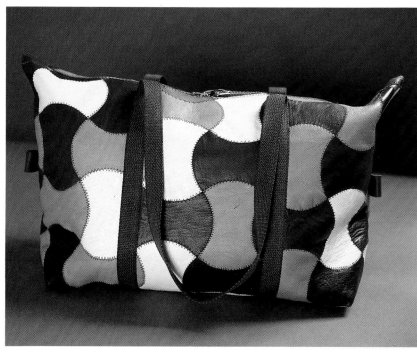

Diagram 1

Method for preparing a spool template of any size

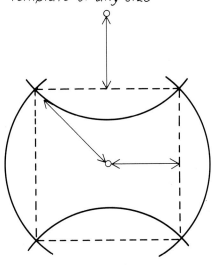

The design is a traditional pattern called Spools and derives its name from the shape of early spools of thread. It is a single shape that interlocks. Two templates are given, based on a 3 inch (75 millimetre) and 4 inch (100 millimetre) square.

The Spool shape can easily be drafted in any size (diagram 1). Choose a larger or smaller size square and draw it on graph paper. Set a compass to the distance between the centre of the square and one corner and place the point of the compass in the centre of the square. Draw an arc across one side of the square, then the opposite side. Now position the point of the compass half the length of a side outside the mid-point of one of the remaining sides, and draw an arc inside the square. Repeat from the corresponding point outside the remaining side of the square. The four arcs form the outline of the template.

Using one of the patterns provided, or your own, MAKE TEMPLATES. Note that no seam allowance is required.

Place the template on the right side of the leather and draw around it with ballpoint pen. Cut out the required number of patches, cutting just inside the ballpoint line. Make sure that your cutting line is smooth

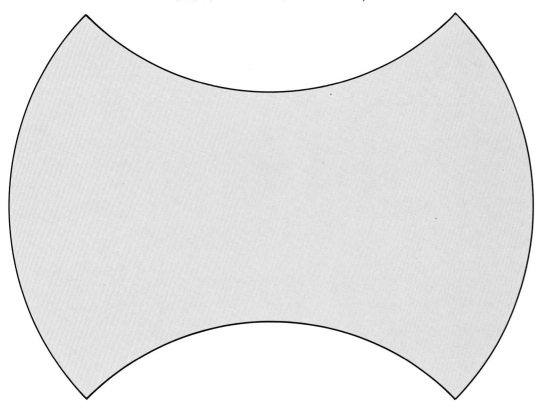

and accurate because the patches will not butt together neatly unless the template and the cutting are absolutely precise.

Lay out a row of patches, alternately horizontal and vertical, which is a little wider than the width of the pattern piece (diagram 2). Pick up two patches from one end of the row and sew the butted edge together using a zigzag or three-step zigzag stitch. Experiment with offcuts to find the best stitch and machine setting. Secure the seam by backstitching for a short distance at the beginning and end of the seam. Add the remainder of the patches until the row is complete. Make up the next row in the same manner. Join the rows by laying the work on a flat surface and butting the rows together. Hold in place with lengths of masking tape, and sew the rows together, matching seams. Continue in this way until a large enough piece has been made.

If you wish to reinforce and line the patchwork, lay the leather face down and spray the wrong side with aerosol adhesive. Cut a piece of lining fabric larger than the leather and smooth it over the adhesive coating. Leave to dry, then cut out according to pattern and make up the bag.

Diagram 2
Join spools to form rows

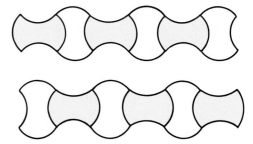

Diamond Patchwork Bags

MAKE TEMPLATE in the size of your choice from the patterns given. The large bags were made with template C and the clutch purse with template B, but any of the other sizes would be equally suitable.

Cut out diamonds from the leather, preferably with a rotaty cutter and ruler, because it produces a smooth, straight-cut edge, which is important when pieces are butted.

Cut a piece of tulle or similar material larger than the bag size. Glue the diamonds to the tulle backing. Position them in rows of contrasting colours, or randomly. The glue holds the diamonds in place while they are positioned and stitched, but it is the stitching that secures them in the finished article, so the glue used need not provide a permanent bond.

Continue adding diamonds until they cover a rectangle equal in width to the desired width of the bag, and twice the desired depth, allowing for seams. For example, the bags shown were made from rectangles measuring 26 × 15 inches (660 × 380 millimetres), 22½ × 14 inches (570 × 355 millimetres) and 11 × 12½ inches (280 × 320 millimetres). The edges can be filled in with half diamonds to produce a straight edge, or full diamonds can be used and the edges cut back to a straight edge.

Stitch the diamonds in place using a zigzag stitch that is wide enough to secure the edges of both adjacent diamonds and with stitches quite close. Sew along the diagonal line between rows of diamonds, working across the rectangle in one direction, then sew the diagonal lines in the other direction (diagram 3).

The diamond patchwork can now be made up into a bag using any pattern. The illustrated bags simply had a zip inserted between the top edges, the side seams sewn and handles attached (except on the clutch purse). The black/cream/rust bag was made from a lightweight leather so the lower ends of the side seams were boxed, but heavier leathers are too bulky to permit this. It is easier to insert the zip between two 1 inch (25 millimetre) wide strips of webbing or soft leather, then sew the edges of the strips to the top edges of the bag, overlapping the raw edge of the bag with the strips. Position a strip to one top edge of the bag with glue, then stitch. Position the other side, glue and stitch with the zip open, from the open end.

For the handles, cut four strips of leather 34 × 1 inch (860 × 25 millimetres) for long handles or 23 × ¾ inch (580 × 20 millimetres) for short handles. (If you have a limited quantity of leather, cut two strips of leather and two lengths of webbing of the same width and matching colour and use the webbing for the inside of the handles.) Place the leather strips wrong sides together and stitch close to each long edge. Before stitching the side seams, position the handles and glue the lower 2 inches (50 millimetres) in place. Stitch to the bag.

Diagram 3

Direction of stitching

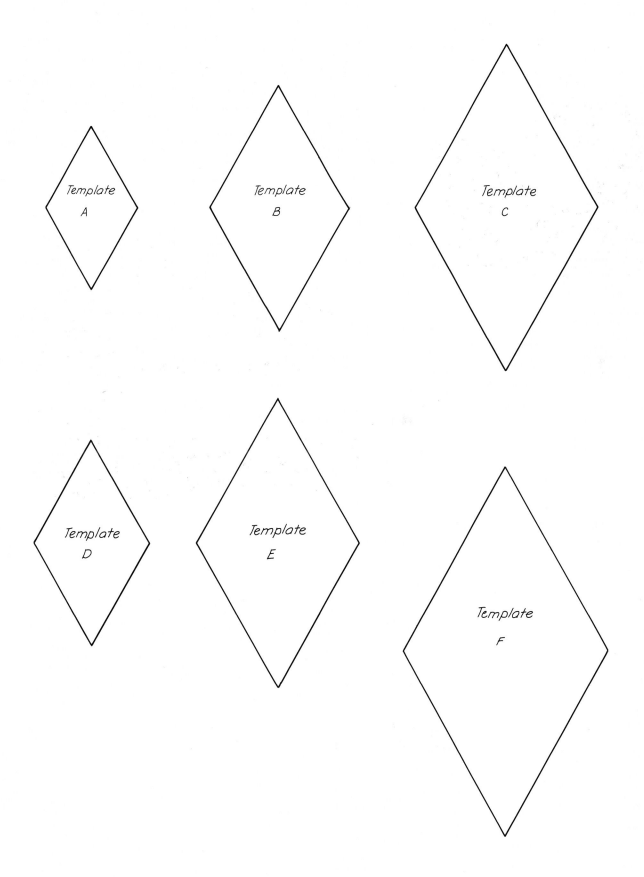

Template
A

Template
B

Template
C

Template
D

Template
E

Template
F

SEWING BOX

There is a place for all your sewing equipment in this attractive and functional soft-sided fabric box.

Finished size: 14 × 7 × 4 inches (350 × 180 × 100 millimetres)

MATERIALS

2/3 yard (61 centimetres) of outer fabric 45 inches (115 centimetres) wide
2/3 yard (61 centimetres) of lining
22 inch (56 centimetre) square of batting
22 inch (56 centimetre) square of needlepunch
7/8 yard (80 centimetres) covered piping or other trim
1 button
28 inches (71 centimetres) of ¼ inch (6 millimetre) elastic
Small quantity of polyester fill for pin cushion

METHOD

Cut from lining fabric:
  1 piece in the box pattern shape
  1 strip of 21 × 4 inches (533 × 100 millimetres)
  1 strip of 13¼ × 4¼ inches (337 × 108 millimetres)
  2 strips of 8 × 4¼ inches (203 × 109 millimetres)
  1 strip 6½ × 5½ inches (165 × 140 millimetres)
  2 squares 3½ × 3½ inches (90 × 90 millimetres)
¼ inch (6 millimetre) seams are allowed throughout.

Pincushion
Sew the two 3½ inch (90 millimetre) squares together, right sides facing, leaving an opening large enough to turn out and fill with polyester. Slipstitch the opening. The pincushion is attached to the lid after the box has been constructed.

Thread pockets
Take the 21 × 4 inch (533 × 100 millimetre) strip and, measuring in from the ¼ inch (6 millimetre) seam line, divide into five, and finger press or iron, as these creases will be sewing guide lines. Turn down 1 inch (25 millimetres), fold under the raw edge, and sew to make a casing for the elastic.

Divide the long side of the box lining, under the lid section, into five, and mark as above.

Place the raw edge of the pocket strip, right sides facing, ¼ inch (6 millimetres) above the line marked "fold and stitch" and sew along this seam line, taking tucks so that the two sets of guide lines match. Insert a 13 inch (330 millimetre) length of elastic in the casing (diagram 1).

Turn the pocket strip up. Sew to the lining along the pressed guide lines, making five pockets (diagram 2).

On the 13¼ × 4¼ inch (337 × 108 millimetre) piece, neaten one long edge by folding over ¼ inch (6 millimetres) twice and sewing. Attach the pocket to the opposite side of the lining to the elasticized pockets, in the same way. Turn up and stitch to the lining down the middle, making two straight pockets (diagram 3).

Side pockets
To make the two side pockets, use the 8 × 4¼ inch (203 × 109 millimetre) pieces. Make a casing for the elastic as for the thread pockets. Attach in a similar fashion to the other pockets, taking tucks to fit the lining. Thread through 6¼ inches (160 millimetres) of elastic. Turn up towards edge of box (diagram 4).

Ruler or pencil pocket
Use the 6½ × 5½ inch (165 × 140 millimetre) piece for this pocket. Neaten along one 6½ inch (165 millimetre) edge. Press back the seam allowance of ¼ inch (6 millimetres) on the other three sides and sew onto lining lid 1¼ inches (32 millimetres) in from edges (diagram 5).

Scissors pocket
The strip for the scissors is 2¾ × 1¼ inches (70 × 32 millimetres). Sew into a tunnel, right sides together with a ¼ inch (6 millimetre) seam. Pull

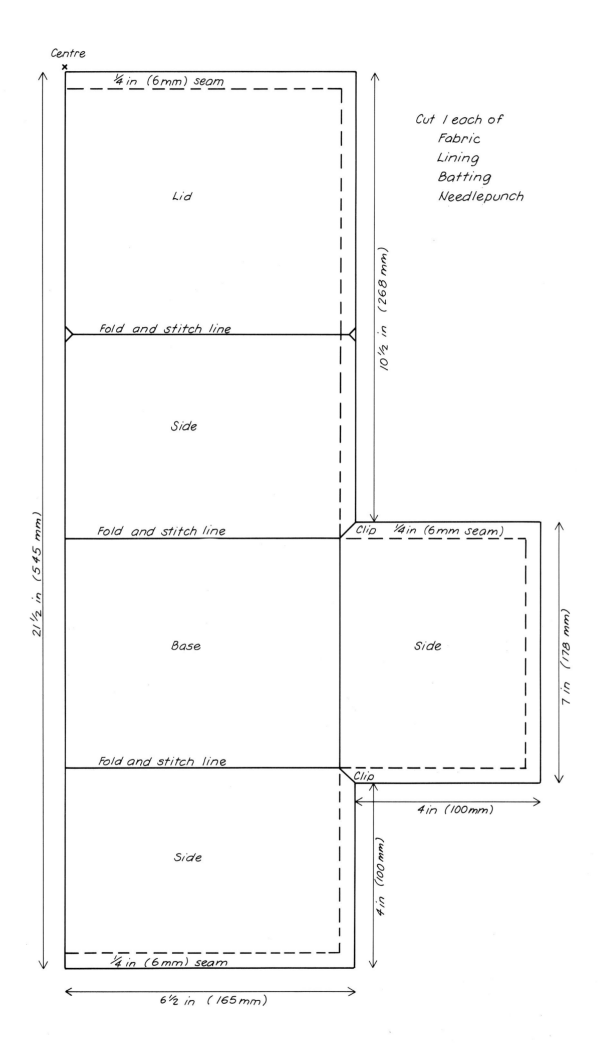

Centre
×

¼ in (6mm) seam

Lid

Fold and stitch line

Side

10½ in (268 mm)

Cut 1 each of
Fabric
Lining
Batting
Needlepunch

Fold and stitch line   Clip   ¼ in (6mm seam)

Base

Side

7 in (178 mm)

Fold and stitch line   Clip

4 in (100mm)

Side

4 in (100 mm)

21½ in (545 mm)

¼ in (6mm) seam

6½ in (165mm)

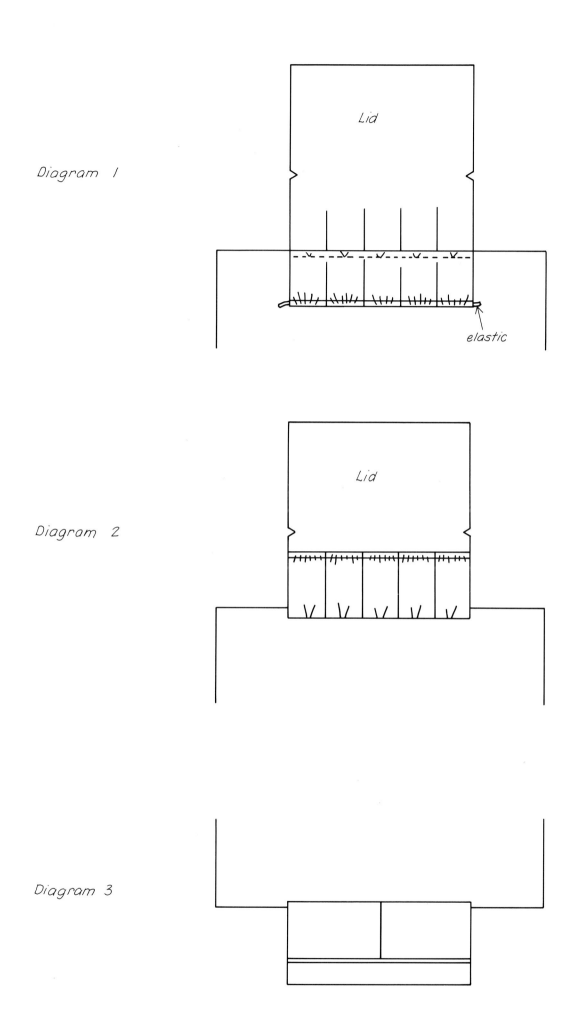

Diagram 1

Lid

elastic

Diagram 2

Lid

Diagram 3

Diagram 4

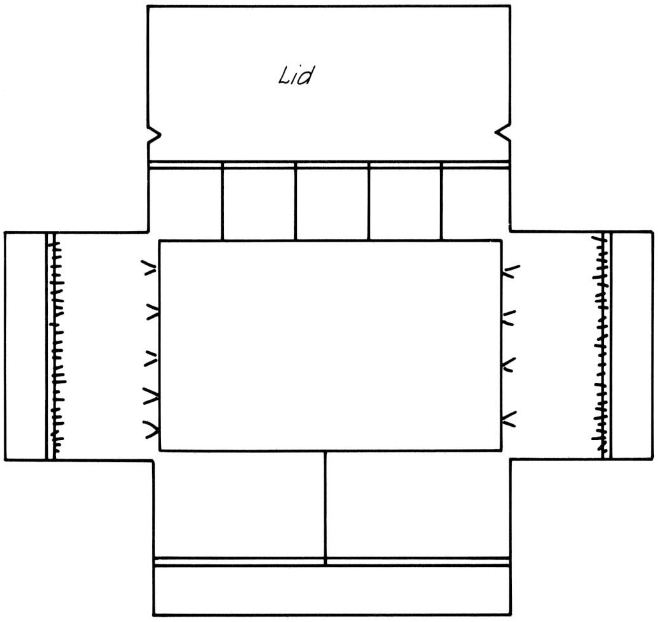

Lid

Diagram 5

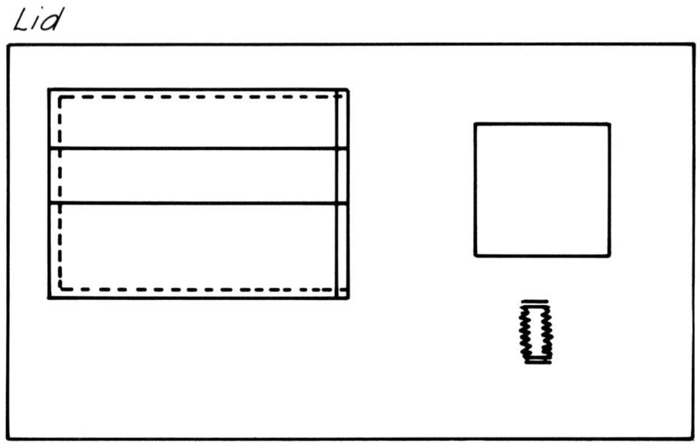

Lid

Diagram 6

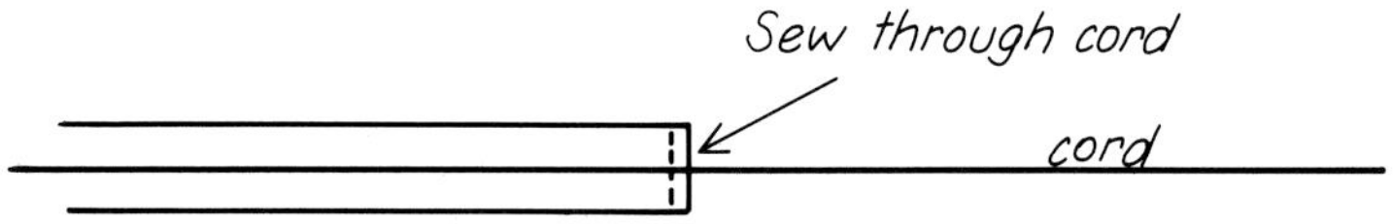

Sew through cord

cord

Diagram 7
Lining

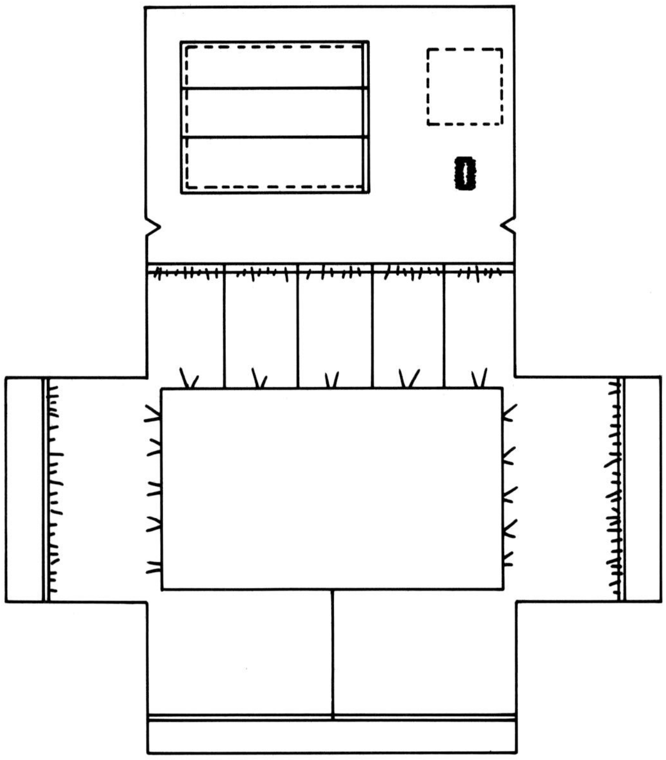

Diagram 8

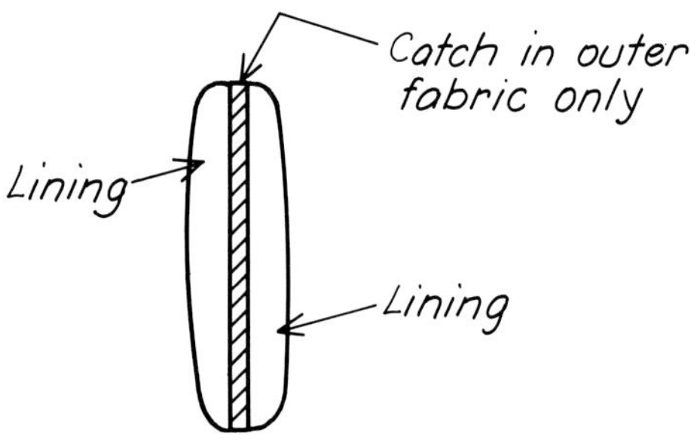

Catch in outer fabric only

Lining

Lining

through to the right side and thread 2 inches (50 millimetres) of elastic through and fasten the elastic securely at each end. Turn under each end and sew as positioned on diagram 5. If you do not possess one of those handy gadgets with a hook on the end for pulling through such narrow tunnels (a loop turner), here is a tip to help do this. Have a piece of cord, twice as long as the tunnel to be turned. Lay the cord over the right side of the fabric from the halfway point of the cord, so that half of the cord is overhanging. Sew through the cord at the top end of the fabric (diagram 6). Fold the fabric right sides together and stitch with zipper foot, not catching in the cord. Pull the fabric over the protruding piece of cord, unpick the sewing on the cord and pull it out of the tunnel. The tunnel will now be turned to the right side with the stitching undamaged.

The completed lining
The lining should now look like diagram 7. Note that the pincushion is attached after completion of the sewing box. Otherwise its bulk could make it difficult to pull all the layers through to the right side when they are sewn together.

To assemble the four layers

Cut out the pattern in the outer fabric, needlepunch and batting. Place the batting next to the wrong side of the outer fabric and then the needlepunch on top. Tack, or zigzag, round the edge of these three layers. Attach the trim round the lid from notch to notch.

Place the right side of the lining to the right side of the outer fabric and sew all round, leaving a 6 inch (150 millimetre) gap for turning. Clip the seams and turn. Slipstitch the gap.

Stitch around the base of the pockets through all thicknesses, making sure the bobbin thread matches the outer fabric.

With the right sides together, bring the sides of the box up and topstitch by hand, catching in the outer fabric only. This makes a very neat finish to the inside of the box and the lining stays in place very well (diagram 8).

Turn the box right side out, sew the pin cushion by the four corners to the lid, and to finish sew a button and loop to the middle edge of the lid.

This bag is an asset for anyone who likes to carry some sewing with them to make use of any spare time. Sewing equipment is held securely in pockets, leaving the main part of the bag to hold the work in progress.

Finished size: 12 × 14 inches (305 × 360 millimetres)

MATERIALS

Two pieces of firm fabric 13 × 15 inches (333 × 380 millimetres) for front and back

Two handles of outer fabric 13 × 3 inches (330 × 76 millimetres)

½ yard (46 centimetres) of printed fabric for lining

Two pieces of iron-on interfacing 13 × 15 inches (330 × 380 millimetres)

14 inches (360 millimetres) of ¼ inch (6 millimetre) elastic

A piece of heavy cardboard 2½ × 10½ inches (65 × 270 millimetres)

Scraps of fabric for Windmill patchwork on the outer pocket

A piece of fabric 10¾ × 15 inches (275 × 380 millimetres) to back the patchwork pocket

A scrap of batting 26 × 3 inches (660 × 76 millimetres) to line the handles (optional)

METHOD

Lining

Cut two pieces 13 × 15 inches (330 × 380 millimetres) from the lining fabric. Sew or press the interfacing to the lining front and back. Stitch the pockets to the lining as shown in diagram 1.

For the thread pocket, cut a piece of lining fabric 6 × 21 inches (150 × 530 millimetres). Fold in half lengthwise – 3 × 21 inches (75 × 530 millimetres). Make a casing for the elastic below the fold and sew to the lining, right sides together, 4½ inches (115 millimetres) from the top, taking tucks on the bottom edge (diagram 2).

Turn the pocket up, thread the 14 inch (360 millimetre) length of ¼ inch (6 millimetre) elastic through the casing. Stitch the pocket to the sides of the lining, and tack the pocket in three places along the top (diagram 3).

Using 5/8 inch (16 millimetre) seam, sew the back and front lining, right sides together, down both sides and along the bottom, leaving a 4 inch (100 millimetre) opening to pull the tote through later (see below).

Box the bottom corners by folding the lining as in diagram 4 and sewing across 1½ inches (40 millimetres) from the point on the wrong side. Trim the point off.

To construct the Windmill patchwork pocket

MAKE TEMPLATES, cut out the fabric and MACHINE PIECE the block, referring to diagram 5 for piecing instructions. Note that the block should measure 8½ inches (216 millimetres) when pieced.

To bring the block up to the width of the tote, add a strip 4 × 8¾ inches (102 × 223 millimetres) to each side of the block. In addition to this, add a strip 2¼ × 15 inches (60 × 380 millimetres) along the bottom. This was not done in the illustrated tote bag, the result being that part of the Windmill block design disappeared under the bottom of the bag when the ends were boxed.

Cut a piece of lining fabric to fit the patchwork pocket, and a binding strip on the straight grain of the fabric 2 × 15 inches (50 × 380 millimetres).

Place the pocket and backing pieces wrong sides together. Fold the binding strip in two lengthwise and sew the raw edge to the top of the pocket in a ¼ inch (6 millimetre) seam. Turn the binding to the back of the pocket and slipstitch.

To construct the outer bag

Cut two pieces 13 × 15 inches (330 × 380 millimetres) of the outer fabric for the front and back. Cut two handles of the outer fabric 13 × 3 inches (330 × 76 millimetres).

Place the patchwork outer pocket on the right side of the tote front piece, and machine baste down the sides and along the bottom.

Place the strip of batting, if it is being used, down the centre of the wrong side of the handle strips and overlap in the middle. Zigzag down the centre raw edge of both handles. The batting insert makes for a more comfortable handle. If the batting is not used, stitch each handle together lengthwise on the wrong side. Pull through to the right side and press the seams down the centre.

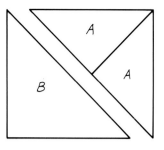

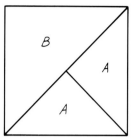

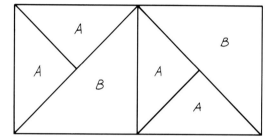

With the right sides together, stitch each end of one handle to the tote front 2½ inches (60 millimetres) either side of the centre point. Repeat with the second handle.

With the right sides together, stitch the sides and bottom of the outer bag with a ½ inch (12 millimetre) seam. Box the bottom corners as in diagram 4. Trim the points off.

With the right sides together, sew the lining to the outside of the tote using a ½ inch (12 millimetre) seam, making sure the handles are inside. Pull through the 4 inch (100 millimetre) opening. Stitch the opening. Cover the piece of cardboard with lining fabric and place in the bottom of the tote.

¼ in (6mm) seam allowance

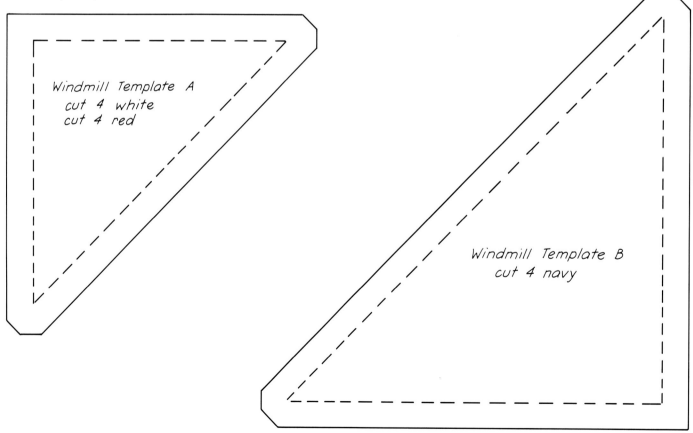

Windmill Template A
cut 4 white
cut 4 red

Windmill Template B
cut 4 navy

Diagram 1

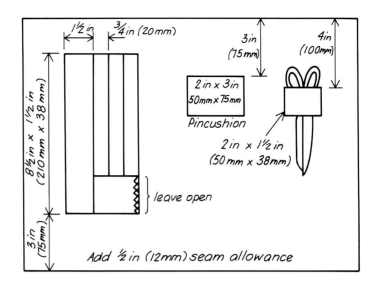

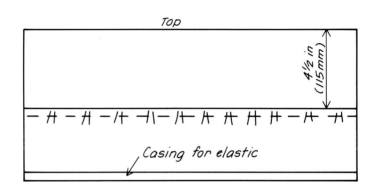

$1\frac{1}{2}$ in $\frac{3}{4}$ in (20mm)

3 in (75mm)   4 in (100mm)

$8\frac{1}{2}$ in x $1\frac{1}{2}$ in (210mm x 38mm)

2 in x 3 in 50mm x 75mm
Pincushion

2 in x $1\frac{1}{2}$ in (50mm x 38mm)

} leave open

3 in (75mm)

Add $\frac{1}{2}$ in (12mm) seam allowance

Diagram 2

Top

$4\frac{1}{2}$ in (115mm)

Casing for elastic

Diagram 3

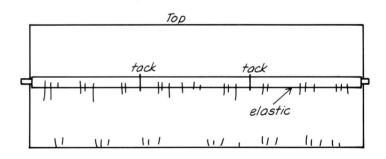

Top

tack   tack

elastic

Diagram 4

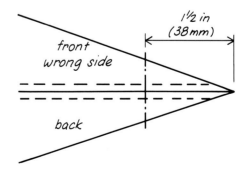

$1\frac{1}{2}$ in (38mm)

front
wrong side

back

PART THREE

QUILTMAKING TECHNIQUES

The first step in any quilting project is to make the templates (unless they have been purchased ready-made). If they are not made accurately, the project is doomed from the start. It is essential to check the accuracy of the templates against the original, and perhaps by assembling one block, before cutting out all the pieces required.

Templates can be made from cardboard or template plastic. The plastic is more durable if the template is to be used repeatedly, but cardboard can be used for a large project if several templates are made, and discarded when they become worn. Geometric shapes can be drawn accurately on graph paper, which is then glued onto a sheet of cardboard, before cutting out the templates. Wait until the glue is completely dry, then cut out exactly on the lines marked on the graph paper. A craft knife or rotary cutter and a metal or sturdy plastic ruler will cut much more precisely than scissors. Patterns can also be traced onto lightweight paper and glued onto the card. Plastic has many advantages for template making: patterns can be traced directly onto the plastic and the templates produced are very durable. It is also very helpful to be able to see the fabric through the template because then the template can be aligned with the grain or stripes, or centred over a motif in the fabric. Template plastic can be purchased from specialty patchwork shops. If you have access to unexposed X-ray film, it can be used for templates although it is not as good as the plastic because it is a little too thin.

Hand and machine piecing require different types of template. For hand piecing, the *sewing line* must be marked accurately on the fabric so the templates are cut to the finished size of the patch. The template is then placed face down on the wrong side of the fabric and a pencil line is drawn around the template. The pieces are cut out adding a ¼ inch (6 millimetre) seam allowance judged by eye. Machine piecing requires an accurate *cutting line* which is used to guide the outer edge of the presser foot. The seam allowance is, therefore, added to the pattern before cutting the templates. Window templates are dual purpose: they have a cut-out area inside the sewing line and include the seam allowance, so either sewing or cutting lines, or both, can be marked.

Label the templates with the pattern name, the piece identification and the grain line. If a piece is to be reversed, indicate this on the template. It is a good idea, particularly with curved seam lines, to cut tiny notches in the template edges where they must meet, so that a pencil mark can be made in the seam allowance to guide the piecing.

Ready-made templates can be purchased, including metal ones, which will obviously last indefinitely. You can expect purchased templates to be absolutely accurate – if not, complain!

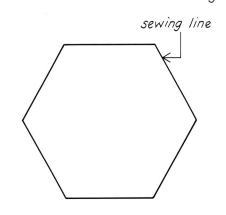

Hand-piecing template
Add seam allowance when cutting
sewing line

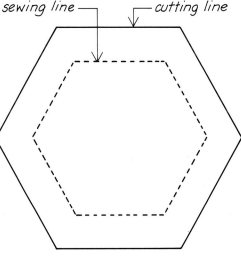

Machine-piecing template
Includes seam allowance
sewing line — — *cutting line*

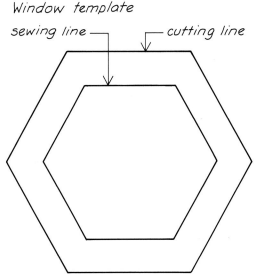

Window template
sewing line — — *cutting line*

Planning the size of the quilt

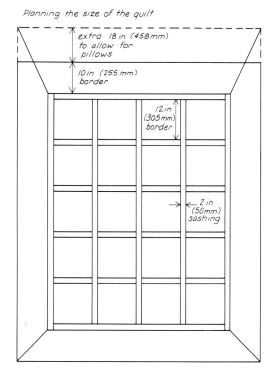

extra 18 in (458mm) to allow for pillows

10 in (255 mm) border

12 in (305mm) border

2 in (50mm) sashing

A question very frequently asked of patchwork shop owners is: "How can I be sure my quilt is going to fit my bed?" This is not so very difficult. First of all decide the type of quilt you want. Do you want it to reach the floor, or just extend far enough to cover the top of a valance? Having established this, take a pencil, paper and tape measure and measure the depth of overhang required, from the edge of the bed. Double this measurement and add it to the width of the bed. Now add the measured depth of the overhang to the length of the bed, plus 18 to 20 inches (460–510 millimetres) to allow for the amount tucked under the pillows. You may prefer to simply cover the pillows with the quilt, without tucking it under them, in which case add only 6 to 10 inches (150–250 millimetres) extra length. Some designs are suitable for tucking under the pillows, others lose their effect if part of the design disappears under the pillows. Add a further 4 to 6 inches (100–150 millimetres) on *all* sides for the amount taken up by the quilting. Now you have arrived at the finished measurement for your quilt.

There are a number of advantages in making the quilt long enough to meet the valance rather than the floor. Obviously, it will be smaller and therefore require less time and expense. But a valance will also take all the wear and tear of contact with the floor and scuff marks from shoes, and it can easily be washed, and replaced when worn, thus extending the life of the quilt. A floor-length quilt will need to have the corners rounded at the bottom of the quilt so that it hangs well.

You will see from the diagram that the finished size of the quilt can be varied in three ways: larger or additional blocks, wider sashing or wider borders. The finished size of the quilt in the diagram would be 78 × 110 inches (1.98 × 2.8 metres). The measurements given in the diagram are all finished size, and seams are not included.

The blocks of a quilt can be set together in a variety of ways.

SASHING

Probably the most frequently used method of setting blocks is the addition of sashing, which creates a lattice-work effect. Short sashes (cut to the same length as the side measurement of the block) are sewn to the bottom edges of all blocks, and to the top edges of the blocks in the top row. The blocks are then sewn together to form vertical rows that have a sash between each block. Long sashes (cut to the length of the vertical rows) are then sewn to the left side of every row, and to the right side of the right hand row. The vertical rows are then joined to complete the quilt top. The width of the sashes can be varied, which allows quite a bit of latitude when trying to arrive at a particular measurement for the quilt (diagram 1).

PLAIN BLOCKS

Plain blocks may be alternated with the patchwork blocks. In this case only half the number of patchwork blocks are required and the plain blocks can be quilted in a suitable design (diagram 2).

DIAGONAL SET

Blocks set on the diagonal can look very effective, either set with alternate plain blocks, or all patchwork ones. With diagonal setting, it is necessary to insert triangles along the outside edge to give a straight edge (diagram 3).

EDGE-TO-EDGE

The blocks may be joined edge-to-edge, in which case an interesting secondary design may appear when geometric pieced blocks are used. Your choice of setting method is largely determined by the design of the blocks. Some designs lose their effect if they are set edge-to-edge and require either sashing or alternate plain blocks. Other designs do not emerge until they are joined edge-to-edge, such as Double Irish Chain, and their design must not be interrupted by sashing (diagram 5).

Setting the blocks
Diagram 1

Diagram 2

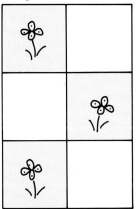

Diagram 3

Diagram 4

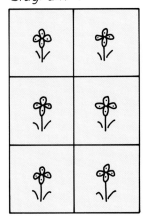

103

Eccentric Star Block
Diagram 5

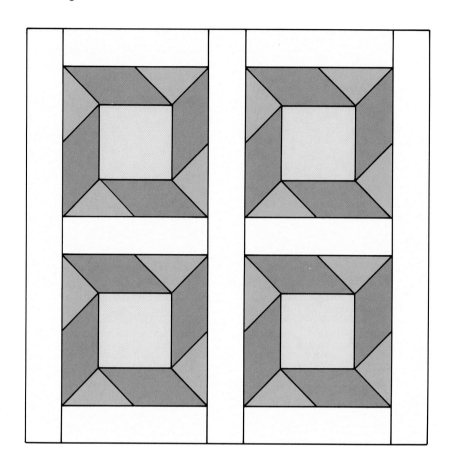

Many quilts are enhanced by the addition of a border that frames the design. Borders also provide an area that shows off an elaborate quilting design, especially if the border is a plain area surrounding the central design. Use of a border will increase the size of the quilt without requiring additional pieced blocks.

Two or more borders may be used. If you use extra borders, vary their width. The combination of 2 inch and 5 inch (50 and 130 millimetre) borders will give a more pleasing appearance than two 3 inch (80 millimetre) borders.

Although the borders are the last pieces added to the quilt, it is preferable to plan and cut them first, especially if the fabric chosen for the border is also to be used in the design. If the patchwork pieces are cut first without thought, it may not be possible to cut the required length for the border from the remaining fabric, and borders should not contain joins. So cut the borders from the length of the fabric before cutting any other pieces from that fabric. It is also wise to allow extra length as a precaution.

STRAIGHT BORDERS

This is the most straightforward type of border. Cut two strips the length of the short sides of the quilt in the desired width. Sew these to the top and bottom of the quilt. To avoid a rippled effect when attaching any type of border, sew with the border fabric on top and hold the fabric so that a little tension is created. If sewn with the quilt on top, the edges of the blocks can easily stretch, gathering in the border fabric which will look rippled. Press the borders, turning the seam toward the border. Cut two more strips the length of the quilt plus the top and bottom borders, and sew to the sides of the quilt. Press. (See diagrams 1 and 2.)

MITRED BORDERS

A mitred border looks very professional and is not difficult to sew. Cut four border strips, allowing generous extra length for the mitre. Mark the centre of each strip and pin to the sides of the quilt, matching centres. Sew one strip to each side of the quilt, beginning and ending the stitching ¼ inch (6 millimetres) from the edge of the quilt. With the wrong side facing, at one corner lay one border over the other. Using a 45 degree set square, draw a line from the end of the stitching to the outer edge of the border (diagrams 3–7). Reverse the two borders so that the other one is now on top and repeat the process. Pin the two borders right sides together, matching pencil lines and sew along the lines. Trim excess fabric, leaving ¼ inch (6 millimetre) seam allowance and press open. Press from the right side also. Repeat at each corner.

Diagram 1

Diagram 2

Mitred borders
Diagram 3

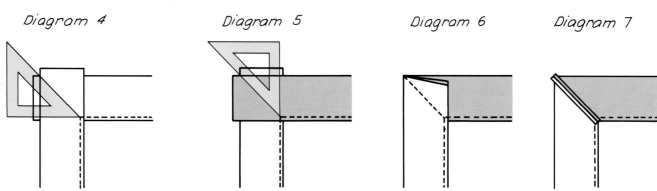

Diagram 4   Diagram 5   Diagram 6   Diagram 7

Square corner borders

Diagram 8

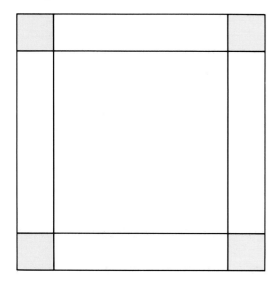

SQUARE CORNER BORDERS

This type of border has a square of contrasting fabric in each corner (diagram 8). It was frequently used by Amish quilters. Cut two border strips the length of the top and bottom edges and sew to the quilt. Cut two more border strips, each slightly longer than the remaining sides of the quilt. Cut four squares of contrasting fabric the size of the width of the border strip, including seam allowances. Sew one square to the top end of the border strip. Sew the strip to the side of the quilt, matching the seam joining the square and border to the seam joining the top of the quilt and the border. Stop sewing a short distance before the lower edge. Trim the border level with the lower border seam, adding a seam allowance. Sew another square to the lower edge of the border strip and then continue sewing the border to the quilt, matching the seams. Repeat on the remaining side.

A bias-bound edge is the recommended finish for a quilt because it is durable and looks neat and attractive. The edges of the quilt receive considerable wear, especially if it is floor length, so a double thickness binding is best for bed quilts, but single binding is sufficient for wall quilts.

TO CUT BIAS STRIPS

Fold the fabric on the true bias by lining up the cut edge with the selvedge. Fold again, matching the folds. Mark the fabric into strips of the desired width, beginning from one of the folded edges (diagram 1). Cut into strips. Sew the strips together to form one long strip (diagram 2). Press the seams open. For single binding, cut strips four times the desired finished width, plus ¼ inch (6 millimetres). For double binding, cut strips six times the desired finished width, plus ½ inch (12 millimetres). So if you want a ½ inch (12 millimetre) binding, cut the strips 2¼ inches (55 millimetres) wide for single binding and press under ½ inch (12 millimetres) on one edge, or for double binding cut the strips 3½ inches (90 millimetres) wide and fold in half. The extra width added after multiplying by four or six allows for the thickness of the quilt.

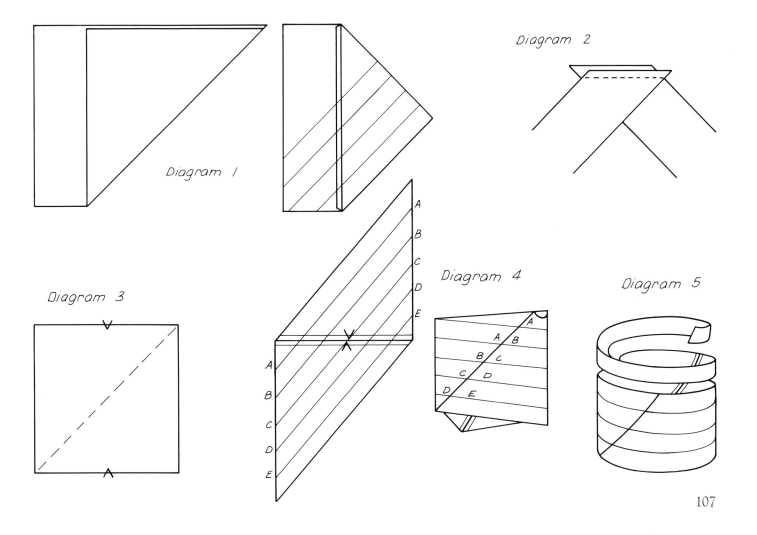

Diagram 1

Diagram 2

Diagram 3

Diagram 4

Diagram 5

Diagram 6

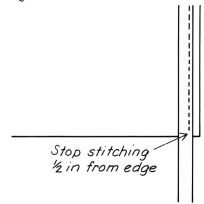

Stop stitching ½ in from edge

Diagram 7

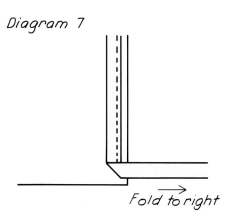

Fold to right

Diagram 8

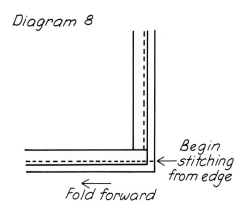

Begin stitching from edge

Fold forward

Diagram 9

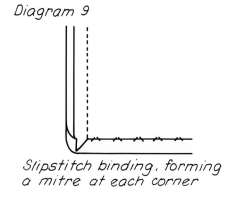

Slipstitch binding, forming a mitre at each corner

TO MAKE CONTINUOUS BIAS

Cut a large square of fabric. Mark the centre on opposite edges. Fold in half diagonally, and press lightly (diagram 3). Cut apart on the fold line. Join the two triangles, matching the centre marks. Press the seam open, and mark strips parallel to the bias edge. Stitch the straight edges together, with the strip marks offset by one width (diagram 4). Cut along the marked lines to form one continuous bias strip (diagram 5). For double binding, fold the strip in half lengthways, and press.

TO ATTACH BIAS BINDING

Pin the binding to the quilt top, beginning in the centre of one side and leaving 6 inches (150 millimetres) free. Stitch the binding to the quilt with a seam allowance equal in width to the finished depth of the binding, which is usually ½ inch (12 millimetres). A ¼ inch (6 millimetre) seam could be used regardless of the width of the binding, but if a seam allowance is used that is the same depth as the binding, the wider seam allowance will pad the binding giving an attractively firm and rounded appearance. Stitch the binding to the quilt, stopping exactly ½ inch (12 millimetres) from the edge (if using a ½ inch (12 millimetre) seam). Backstitch and trim the threads. (See diagram 6.)

Fold the binding to the right, at right angles to the seam, forming a diagonal fold (diagram 7). Press the fold lightly, then fold the binding forward, aligning the folded edge with the edge of the quilt (diagram 8). Begin stitching again at the raw edge and continue to the next corner. Repeat the process.

When you have almost reached the binding that was left free at the beginning, stop stitching and remove the work from the machine. Seam the ends of the binding, then finish stitching it to the quilt.

Press the binding away from the quilt top and fold it over the raw edge to the back. A mitre will form on the front at each corner. Fold the binding so that another mitre forms on the back. Slipstitch the binding to the back of the quilt, taking a few stitches in each mitre to hold it in place (diagram 9).

The finished quilt is made up of three layers: backing fabric, batting and the quilt top. These layers must be basted with thread or safety pins before the edges of the quilt are finished and the quilting done. The process of assembling the layers can be very tedious, but it is most important because if it is not done well the completed quilt will be wrinkled and puckered. The method described is used by both the authors and is guaranteed to be worth the effort involved.

A large carpeted area of floor is required because the layers are pinned to the carpet so that there is no movement of the layers while the basting or pinning is done. A table or hard floor is not suitable.

Mark the centres of the four sides of the top, batting and backing to help align the layers correctly. You will need plenty of strong pins, preferably a heavier weight than dressmaking pins, and plenty of medium-size safety pins.

Spread the backing fabric out on the carpet, wrong side up. Fasten it to the carpet along one end, by pushing the pins in at an angle. Repeat this at the opposite end, keeping the backing taut. This whole process is greatly simplified if you can persuade a friend to help by working on the opposite side. Then push the pins in along one side, and repeat for the opposite side, once again keeping the fabric taut.

Place the batting on top of the backing, using the marked centre lines as a guide. Make sure that there are no wrinkles, but do not stretch the batting. Pin to the carpet through the backing.

Centre the quilt top over the other two layers, using the guide lines previously marked. Pin, repeating the method used for the backing.

The three layers should now be firmly pinned to the carpet with no wrinkles or bulges, ready for basting with thread or safety pins. A medium-size pin is ideal, being large enough to catch all three layers, but not so large that they leave holes in the fabric. Do not be sparing with the safety pins. They should be as close as every 4 inches (100 millimetres). When the entire top has been safety-pinned, remove the straight pins from the carpet, pinning the edges of the three layers with quilter's pins as you do so. Alternatively, the layers may be basted together. Initially, the basting seems very difficult because you must work from the top and cannot have one hand underneath to guide the return of the needle, but it becomes more comfortable with practice. Use a long sturdy needle and a stabbing motion towards the carpet then angle the needle back up to the surface. Start at the centre and work out to each side, then work diagonal lines. Next baste parallel to the edges, spacing the lines about 12 inches (250 millimetres) apart. Finally, baste round the outside edge, removing the pins from the carpet as you stitch. The use of safety pins or basting is a matter of personal preference. Pins are ideal if the quilting is to be done in a large floor frame, but basting may be preferable if a hoop is to be used because the pins could make it difficult to position and adjust the quilt in the hoop.

When basting or pinning is complete, trim the excess backing and batting level with the quilt top. The next step is BINDING THE QUILT, because if the binding is done before the quilting, it saves wear on the raw edges and makes the quilt more comfortable to work on. Then, when the quilting is finished, the quilt is ready for use.

Diagram 1

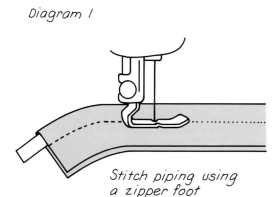

*Stitch piping using
a zipper foot*

Diagram 2

Trim the completed cushion front to the finished size plus ½ inch (12 millimetres) on all sides. Stitch piping to the right side of the front using a zipper foot (diagram 1). Have the piping just inside the seam line. At the corners, clip the seam allowance of the piping and slightly round the corners. Finish the ends of the piping by opening one end and overlapping the fabric (diagram 2).

For the cushion back, cut two pieces of fabric, each the same height as the front and half the width plus 2½ inches (62 millimetres). So if the front is 17 inches (430 millimetres) square (for a finished size of 16 inches or 405 millimetres), the back pieces will be 17 × 11 inches (430 × 280 millimetres).

Press under ½ inch (12 millimetres) on one long edge of each piece, then turn under a 1 inch (25 millimetre) hem and stitch. Sew a strip of velcro along the right side of one hemmed edge and along the wrong side of the other. The velcro need not be a continuous strip—several small pieces could be used instead. Lap one cushion back over the other so that the velcro adheres and baste the overlapped top edges together.

Place the cushion back and front right sides together and stitch around all the edges. Have the wrong side of the front uppermost and stitch, again using a zipper foot, so that the stitching is slightly closer to the piping than the first row of stitching. Open the velcro and turn the cushion to the right side. Press lightly.

Now make a separate case for the cushion filling, which is inserted into the cushion cover. It can then be easily removed when the cover requires washing. Cut two pieces of calico 1 inch (25 millimetres) larger on all sides than the cushion cover. Place the right sides together and stitch around all the edges, leaving an opening for filling. Turn to the right side and fill with polyester or wool. Slipstitch the opening and insert the case into the cushion cover.

An alternative to piping is a bound edge. Make the cushion back as above and place the back and front wrong sides together. Baste. Apply a 2 inch (50 millimetre) bias strip in the same way as when BINDING A QUILT.

Too often women's art has been anonymous, so take pride in your work and get into the habit of signing it. If you also date the work you will find it a useful record of when you made a particular piece. If the quilt is to be a gift, it is much more personal if it is signed and you may also want to record the recipient's name. A quilt given to a baby can have the name and birth date of the child stitched on it as well as your signature.

The signature can be tucked discreetly somewhere on the front or it can be a bold part of the design. You may prefer to put it on the reverse of the quilt, especially if you want to include more lengthy details of time, place and occasion.

It is easier to embroider a signature before the layers are assembled, but it is not too difficult to embroider through a single layer even after the quilting has been done. There are various ways of attaching a signature and message to a quilt.

One is to baste a straight line wherever you wish to place the signature. Write the name directly onto the quilt in pencil and stitch over the pencil line in stem stitch, chain stitch or backstitch. Or you may be able to stitch directly, without a pencil line.

If you want a more exact stitching guide, write the signature on paper and baste it to the quilt. Stitch through the paper and gently tear it away when the embroidery is complete.

You may prefer the precision of counted thread work. One method is to draw up your signature from an alphabet chart on graph paper, then embroider it in either cross-stitch or backstitch on a piece of even-weave fabric. The fabric can then be cut out in the shape of your choice, the raw edges turned under, and the piece slipstitched to the quilt. Alternatively, a piece of embroidery canvas can be basted to the quilt and the embroidery done over the canvas. The canvas is then carefully removed, thread by thread, leaving the embroidery on the quilt.

Cross-stitch and backstitch alphabets are included which can be used to chart your signature and message on graph paper as a guide for stitching. If you prefer free embroidery but would like something more elegant than your normal handwriting, you can trace off a signature from the copper plate and script alphabets.

ABCDEFGHIJKLMN
OPQRSTUVWXYZ
abcdefghijklmnopqrstu
vwxyz
1234567890

ABCDEFGHIJKLMN
OP2RSTUVWXYZ
abcdefghijklmnopqrstuv
wxyzsw
1234567890

ABCDEFGHIJKLMNOP
QRSTUVWXYZ
abcdefghijklmnopqr
stuvwxyz
1234567890

ABCDEFGHIJKLM
NOPQRSTUVWXYZ
abcdefghijklmnop
qrstuvwxyz
1234567890£

Tying is an alternative method of holding the layers of a quilt together. It is much quicker than quilting, and in some cases is the only practical method. For example, if a very thick batting has been used for extra warmth, the thickness makes quilting very difficult, so you may prefer to tie the quilt. Patchwork done with heavyweight materials or onto a backing square may also be better tied than quilted.

The layers of the quilt must still be basted together. The ties may be positioned according to the patchwork design, or it may be necessary to mark evenly spaced points on the quilt top. Traditionally, the ties were visible on the top surface of the quilt for added decoration.

Thread a large-eyed needle with a strong decorative thread such as acrylic yarn, crochet or buttonhole thread or embroidery cotton. Make a stitch from the top through all layers and back to the top, leaving a length of thread to form the tie. The stitch may be repeated for extra strength. Knot the thread ends securely, and trim, leaving a tail about 1 inch (25 millimetres) long. Tufts can be formed by using two or three strands instead of a single thread.

If you wish to tie a quilt but do not want to have visible knots or tufts, you may prefer to work from the backing side and form the knots on the underside so that only the small stitch will show on the top. For barely visible ties which are still secure, use a matching shade of quilting thread, and position the stitches in the seamlines, then tie on the underside.

A light box is most useful when transferrring designs from a pattern to the fabric. It is a shallow box containing a fluorescent light. A sheet of glass or opaque perspex is placed over the box. They are manufactured for photographic and X-ray use, and you may be able to buy one of these, perhaps second-hand.

An improvised light box can also be set up in a number of ways. The simplest is to tape your design to a large window then tape the fabric over it and trace the design. This method is not suitable for large projects because it is very tiring for the arms, but it is useful for small items. If you have a glass-topped coffee table or dining table, it can double as a light box if you place a lamp beneath it. If you have a dining table that can be extended to take an extra section, a sheet of glass or perspex can be placed in the opening and a lamp put underneath.

A light box can be used for tracing quilting designs onto fabric, tracing applique patterns directly onto fabric without cutting a pattern, and positioning applique patches on the background fabric.

Most quilters begin by using a hoop, which has many advantages. It is inexpensive, portable and allows the work to be turned so that the quilter can work in whatever direction is comfortable. The disadvantages are that the position of the hoop must be changed repeatedly as work progresses, and only one person can quilt at a time. A free-standing floor frame reduces the amount of handling the quilt receives and enables several quilters to work together. It is also permanently set up and a spare ten minutes can be spent quilting, where it would not be worth putting the work in a hoop and preparing to quilt for such a short time. The disadvantage of a floor frame is that the position of the quilt is fixed, and all movement must be done by the quilter who will not always be able to sew in her preferred direction. With perseverance, frame quilting does, however, become much more comfortable.

If you would like to try frame quilting but cannot buy a frame in your area, or do not want to outlay a large sum on a frame because you do not do enough quilting to justify the expense, or if you feel unsure about whether you will be happy quilting in a frame, here are instructions for making a very basic frame. It is not at all sophisticated or elegant, but it is easy to make and inexpensive. It will allow you to try quilting in a frame and perhaps buy a more elaborate model later. I began with a frame such as this and even though I now have a superior model, the original frame is still used when I need a second frame. The quilt is attached to two rails, which are braced by two stretcher rails. The four rails are held together by G-clamps and supported by four free-standing supports. Anyone who can make a quilt could make this frame. You will need:

MATERIALS

Dressed timber
Four 30 inch (760 millimetre) lengths of 4 × 2 inch (100 × 50 millimetre)
Sixteen 12 inch (300 millimetre) lengths of 2 × 1 inch (50 × 25 millimetre)
Two 36 inch (910 millimetre) lengths of 2 × 1 inch (50 × 25 millimetre)
Two 8 foot (2.5 metre) lengths of 2 × 1 inch (50 × 25 millimetre)

Four 2 inch (50 millimetre) G-clamps
16 feet (5 metres) of hessian upholstery webbing or nylon webbing

Tools needed
Handsaw, hammer and nails, chisel, staple gun, sandpaper, PVA glue.

METHOD

At one end of each length of 4 × 2 inch (100 × 50 millimetre), make two saw cuts, each 1 inch (25 millimetres) in from the short edge and 2 inches (50 millimetres) deep. Chisel out between the saw cuts to form

Diagram 1

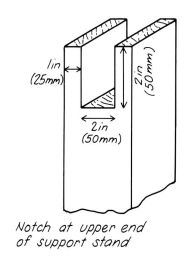

Notch at upper end
of support stand

Diagram 2

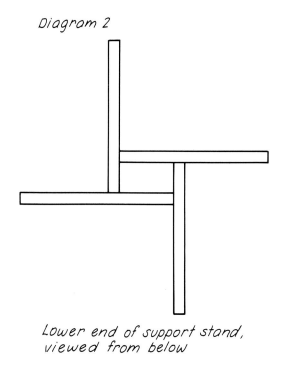

Lower end of support stand,
viewed from below

a notch 2 × 2 inches (50 × 50 millimetres) (diagram 1). Sandpaper the notch smooth.

At the other end of each length of 4 × 2 inch (100 × 50 millimetre), glue and nail four of the 12 inch (300 millimetre) lengths of 2 × 1 inch (50 × 25 millimetre), as shown in diagram 2. Round off the outer ends with coarse sandpaper.

Sand the four rails until smooth. Using a staple gun (or tacks), attach a length of webbing to each of the long rails so that the webbing extends beyond the timber. If the long rails are 8 feet (2.5 metres) long, they will cater for a full size quilt, and you may prefer to use 2 × 2 inch (50 × 50 millimetre) timber. Make the rails shorter if your work is not usually as large as that. It is useful to have several pairs of rails in different lengths, so that a size appropriate to the quilt can be used. If the rails are longer than necessary they take up more room than they need to.

Paint or polyurethane the stands if you wish, but leave the rails as bare wood so that they do not stain the quilt.

HOW TO SET A QUILT INTO THE FRAME

Baste the layers of the quilt as usual. Do not bind the edges of the quilt after the layers have been assembled, as is recommended for hoop quilting. It is always advisable to leave some excess fabric around the lining and borders of a quilt, which can be trimmed off before the quilt is bound. The excess is especially useful when attaching a quilt to a frame because if the quilt is pinned in the extra fabric, holes made by the pins are not a problem.

Mark the centre point on each long rail. Matching centres, pin one side of the quilt to the webbing with 2 inch (50 millimetre) safety pins. A quicker method that can be used if you have allowed excess material is to attach the fabric to the rail, instead of the webbing, using a staple gun. The staples are removed later with a small pair of pliers. If the quilt has already been bound, pin it carefully along the seam line of the binding – don't use staples! Attach the opposite side of the quilt to the other long rail.

Roll the quilt onto the rails so that about 18 inches (450 millimetres) of the quilt top remains exposed. The area not rolled should be the part that will be quilted first, which is usually the centre. If possible, have someone to help roll the quilt so that it is evenly wound, which is difficult to do alone.

Place the short rails (the stretchers) across the ends of the long rails as shown in diagram 3. On one side, fasten the two rails together with G-clamps. (Have the wind-up parts of the clamps underneath so that they are not in the way.) Now attach the stretchers to the rails on the opposite side. Apply tension to the stretchers as you do so, so that the exposed section of the quilt is stretched out flat. It should not be too taut – you will discover as you quilt how much tension to apply. Cut several 12 inch (300 millimetre) lengths of webbing and zigzag or glue the ends to prevent fraying. Wrap around the stretcher rail and attach ends to the quilt with a safety pin to hold the edges of the quilt (diagram 3).

Position the four stands so that they support the protruding ends of either the long rails or the stretchers. The ends of the rails will fit into the notches cut into the upper ends of the stands.

You are now ready to quilt. Use a chair that is a comfortable height. An adjustable typist's chair on castors is perfect because not only can the correct height be set, but you will also be able to swivel to a comfortable angle for the direction of stitching, and roll yourself along as you work across the width of the quilt. Set up a lamp to provide a good working light. When not working on the quilt, cover it with an old sheet to protect it from sunlight and cats who will be convinced that it is a lovely quilted hammock designed especially for them.

Diagram 3

Quilt set into frame ready to be placed on support stands

The only essential materials are needles, thread, scissors and fabric, but many other items of equipment, some of them only recently made available, make quilting easier and more accurate. The items shown in the photograph are:

Quilting hoops. These are available in several sizes. A stand to support the hoop is an optional extra.

Graph paper. Sheets with large squares are particularly useful for designing patchwork blocks.

Quilting pins. Longer than sewing pins, these pins cope well with the bulk of the layers of a quilt.

Bias maker. Bias strips of fabric are threaded through this gadget and ironed as they emerge, producing a bias binding that is ready to use. Available in different widths.

Glue stick. A water-soluble glue can be used to position fabric and to glue paper to cardboard when making templates.

Acu-angle strips (templates). These are useful for fast and accurate cutting of diamond shapes.

Pre-cut papers (paper templates). These are time-saving for precise English piecing.

Quilter's quarter. This is a perspex ¼ inch (6 millimetre) strip used to add the seam allowance to templates, and as a check on seam width.

Leather thimble and open thimble. These are varieties of thimbles that can be used instead of the traditional thimble or on the underneath hand.

Chalk pencils. These come in three colours, complete with eraser and sharpener.

Rotary cutters and spare blades. Rotary cutters are indispensable for fast and exact cutting, especially of strips, borders and bias.

Mat for use with rotary cutters. A self-sealing, non-slip mat, it is also a useful work surface because it grips the fabric.

Purchased templates. In the illustration one example of the many brands available is shown.

Stencils. These have pre-cut quilting designs.

Dressmaker's carbon paper. This is used for transferring designs.

Quilter's square. This is used for marking accurate squares and diagonal and parallel lines.

Quilter's ruler.

BATTING

Batting or *batts* refers to the filler that goes between the face and the backing. Over the years, quilters have used rags, yarns, feathers, raw wool, even cornhusks. But today's batting comes in made-to-measure, easy-to-work sizes and densities.

Wool batting

Several countries now produce a wool batting. The 3 ounce (85 gram) weight is the one deemed most suitable for quilting. There is also a 6 ounce (170 gram) weight, which would be almost impossible to quilt, but it could be tied and would make a very warm bed quilt. Both weights are 59 inches (1.5 metres) wide.

Polyester or Tetron batting

The newest fiber for battings, and the easiest to quilt. It comes in large, seamless sheets, is lightweight, and will not ball or clump after repeated washings. It requires less quilting, since the stitches can be further apart—up to 8 inches. The easiest to use are blankets (72" × 96", 81" × 96", and 90" × 108"), which are treated on both sides with sizing, making them easier to handle and to stitch. Never needs preshrinking.

Cotton batting

Available with smooth, sized surfaces for easy handling, and always purchased preshrunk. The preference of many quilters, because of the look and feel of natural fibers, the drawback is that it will clump inside the quilt after many years of use and repeated washings. The quilting stitches must be closer together, with quilt pockets no larger than 3 inches. *Cotton sheet blankets* and *cotton flannel* may also be used: they provide less loft, moderate warmth, but will not clump.

PART FOUR

GALLERY OF QUILTS

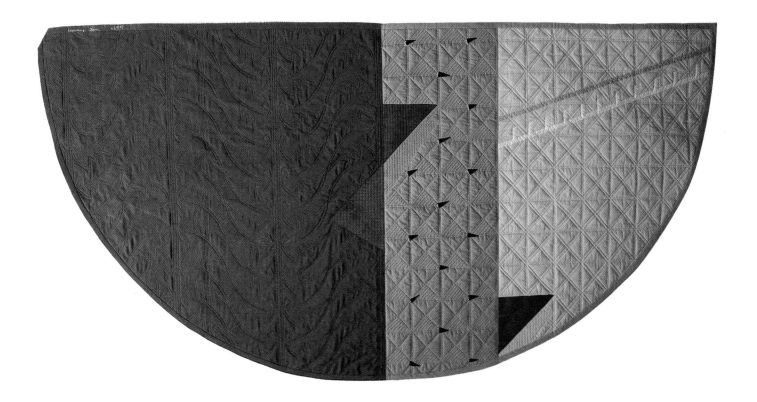

TITLE: *Departing Storm*
QUILTER: Malcolm Harrison
SIZE: 106 inches (diameter) × 52½ inches (radius) (2.68 × 1.33 metres)
CONSTRUCTION: Machine piecing, machine applique, machine quilting
FABRIC: Cotton, plastic and shells
DESIGN: An original design based on the medieval bishop's cope

TITLE: *Quiet Rain*
QUILTER: Malcolm Harrison
SIZE: 94½ inches (diameter) × 47 inches (radius) (2.40 × 1.19 metres)
CONSTRUCTION: Machine piecing, machine applique, machine quilting
FABRIC: Cotton, plastic
DESIGN: An original design based on the medieval bishop's cope

TITLE: *Aloha*
QUILTER: Rosan McLeod
SIZE: 38½ × 68 inches (0.98 × 1.72 metres)
CONSTRUCTION: Hand applique, hand quilting
FABRIC: Cotton
DESIGN: Original

122

TITLE: *Through the Vortex*
QUILTER: Rosan McLeod
SIZE: 56 × 61 inches (1.40 × 1.55 metres)
CONSTRUCTION: Machine piecing, hand quilting
FABRIC: Cotton
DESIGN: Original

These three pieces are examples of work done in Thailand featuring applique and reverse applique. They are stitched by hand and are unquilted.

TITLE: *Day Dream*
QUILTER: Valerie Cuthbert
SIZE: 39 × 50 inches (1 × 1.25 metres)
CONSTRUCTION: Hand and machine piecing, crazywork, embroidery,
three-dimensional flowers with wrapped stems, hand quilting
FABRIC: Cottons and blends
DESIGN: Original

TITLE: *Water Lily*
QUILTER: Valerie Cuthbert
SIZE: 40 × 30 inches (1 × 0.75 metres)
CONSTRUCTION: Machine curved strip piecing
FABRIC: Cottons, blends and dyed fabric
DESIGN: Original

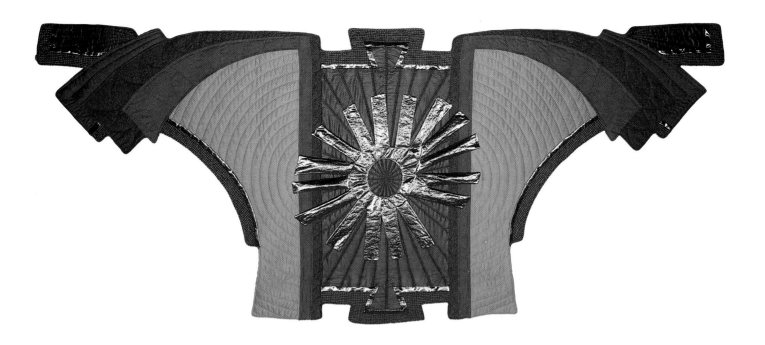

TITLE: *Alkemi*
QUILTER: Barbara Bilyard
OWNER: Mary-Anne Boyd-White
SIZE: 80 × 40 inches (2 × 1 metres)
CONSTRUCTION: Machine piecing, hand quilting
FABRIC: Cotton, parachute cotton and lamé
DESIGN: Original

This quilt was commissioned for the foyer of business premises and
incorporates the company logo.

TITLE: *Voyage to Los Angeles*
QUILTER: Barbara Bilyard
SIZE: 41½ inches (1.05 metres) diameter
CONSTRUCTION: Machine piecing, hand quilting
FABRIC: Cottons, lamé, velvet, moiré, silks, sequin stars and beads
DESIGN: An original design mandala made to celebrate the yacht voyage
from Hawaii to Los Angeles of the quilter's husband.

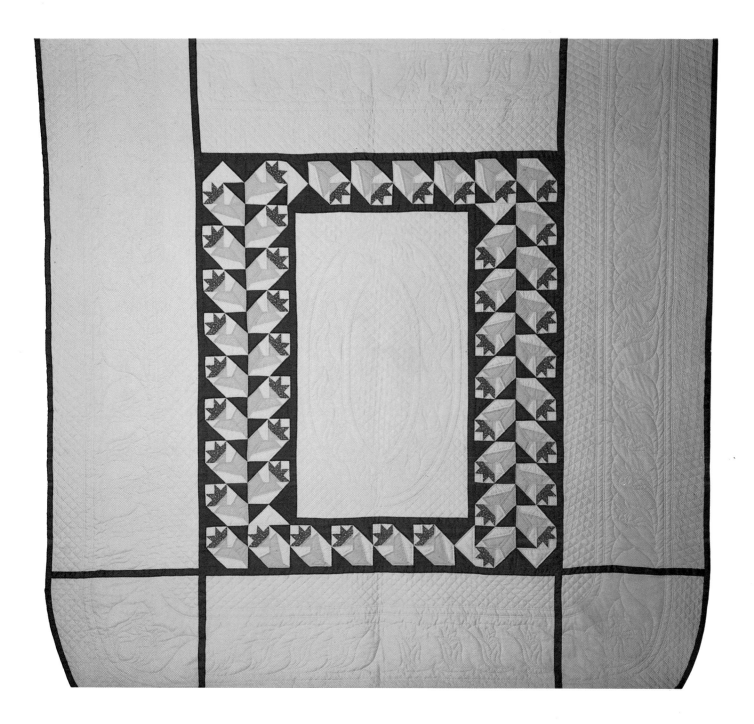

TITLE: *Mountain Lily*
QUILTER: Peigi Martin
OWNERS: Maureen and John Kelly
SIZE: 7 feet 6 inches × 8 feet 6 inches (2.3 × 2.6 metres)
CONSTRUCTION: Machine piecing, hand quilting
FABRIC: Cottons and blends
DESIGN: Adapted from a design by Susie Ennis for the company Quilts
and Other Comforts, Box 394-MLQ, Wheatridge, Colorado, USA 80033.

TITLE: *American Folk Art*
QUILTER: Peigi Martin
OWNERS: Robin and Robyn Martin
SIZE: 7 × 8 feet (2.15 × 2.45 metres)
CONSTRUCTION: Squares of printed fabric have been machine pieced and stab quilted by hand
FABRIC: Printed chintz and cotton blend

TITLE: *Basket Sampler*
QUILTERS: Diane Dolan, Vivien O'Connell, Catherine Cossar-Johnstone, Ngaere McGregor, Juliet Taylor, Louise Porter, Jenny Scott
OWNERS: Stephanie and John Whooley
SIZE: 7 × 7 feet (2.15 × 2.15 metres)
CONSTRUCTION: Hand and machine piecing, hand applique, hand quilting
FABRIC: Cottons and blends
DESIGN: Traditional and original blocks

This is a group quilt made as a wedding gift for the owners. It has been personalized by depicting the occupations of the couple in the blocks—one basket contains a hammer and saw and another contains a blackboard and teacher, representing carpentry and teaching.

TITLE: *Sashiko Moon*
QUILTER: Barbara Bilyard
SIZE: 39 inches (1 metre) diameter
CONSTRUCTION: Machine piecing, hand quilting, sashiko quilting
FABRIC: Kimono fabrics and cottons
DESIGN: Original

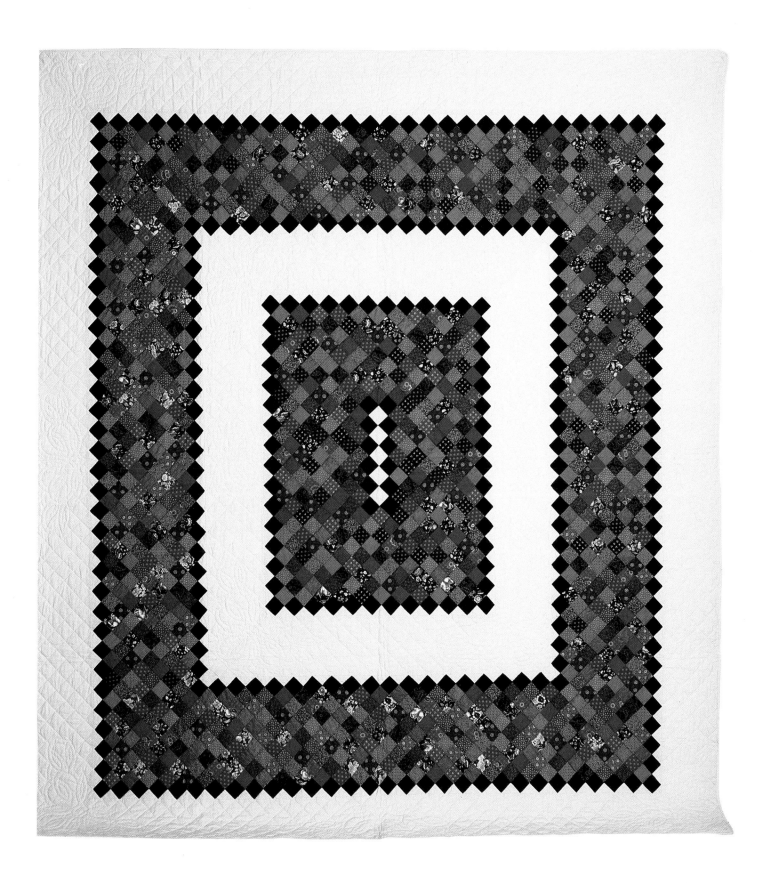

TITLE: *Boston Commons*
QUILTER: Juliet Taylor
OWNER: Louise Porter
SIZE: 90 × 100 inches (2.3 × 2.5 metres)
CONSTRUCTION: Machine piecing, hand quilting
FABRIC: Cottons and blends
DESIGN: Traditional

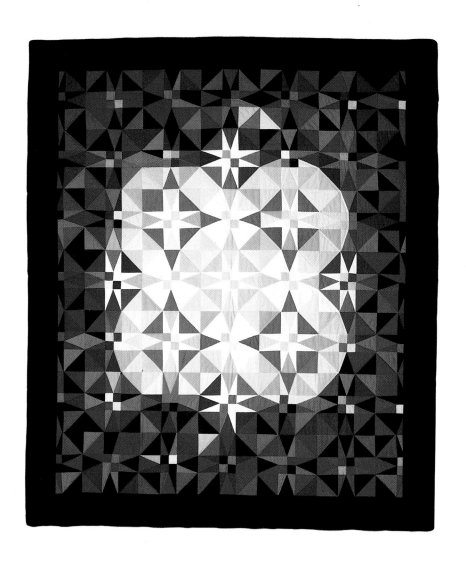

TITLE: *Arabian Nights*
QUILTER: Juliet Taylor
OWNER: Louise Porter
SIZE: 80 × 70 inches (2 × 1.75 metres)
CONSTRUCTION: Machine piecing, hand quilting
FABRIC: Cottons and blends
DESIGN: Adapted from a Jeffrey Gutcheon design

TITLE: *The Charm of Nasturtiums*
QUILTER: Jo Cornwall
OWNER: Juliet Taylor
SIZE: 60 × 60 inches (1.5 × 1.5 metres)
CONSTRUCTION: Hand and machine piecing, hand applique, hand quilting
FABRIC: Cottons and blends
DESIGN: Original design incorporating a traditional charm quilt section

137

TITLE: *Fleur*
QUILTER: Louise Porter
OWNER: Juliet Taylor
SIZE: 40 inches (1 metre) diameter
CONSTRUCTION: English piecing by hand
FABRIC: Liberty prints and cottons
DESIGN: Traditional

TITLE: *Pourangahua Flight*
QUILTER: Barbara Bilyard
SIZE: 47 × 37 inches (1.2 × 0.94 metres)
CONSTRUCTION: Machine piecing, hand quilting, sashiko quilting
FABRIC: Cottons and blends
DESIGN: Taken from a drawing by Theo Schoon. Legend has it that
Pourangahua brought the kumara plant to New Zealand on his magic bird
from its legendary home of Hawaiiki. The border is a traditional Maori
weaving pattern called *aramoana* or 'pathway of the sea'.

TITLE: *New Morning*
QUILTER: Sue Curnow
SIZE: 68 × 60 inches (1.72 × 1.52 metres)
CONSTRUCTION: Machine piecing, hand quilting
FABRIC: Cottons, blends, velvet
DESIGN: Original design based on a traditional block

TITLE: *Kimono Quilt*
QUILTER: Clare Wylie
SIZE: 53 × 31 inches (1.34 × 0.78 metres)
CONSTRUCTION: Machine piecing, hand quilting, sashiko quilting
FABRIC: Cottons and blends
DESIGN: Traditional

Acknowledgements

Our heartfelt thanks to the many quilters who generously entrusted us with their precious quilts for inclusion in the Gallery section; and to Diane Dolan of Patches of Ponsonby for her enthusiasm and assistance with equipment for photography.

As all projects and techniques are illustrated, the illustrations have not been separately indexed. Numbers in **bold** indicate the main reference to the terms given in CAPITALS in the text.